THE FIRST YEAR FOR
ELEMENTARY SCHOOL TEACHERS

Photography by Keith Megay

THE FIRST YEAR FOR ELEMENTARY SCHOOL TEACHERS

A Practical Plan for Dealing with the Short and Long-Term Management of Teaching Duties and Responsibilities

By

KAREN MEGAY-NESPOLI, ED.M.

CHARLES C THOMAS • PUBLISHER
Springfield • Illinois • U.S.A.

Published and Distributed Throughout the World by

CHARLES C THOMAS • PUBLISHER
2600 South First Street
Springfield, Illinois 62794-9265

© *1993 by* CHARLES C THOMAS • PUBLISHER

ISBN 0-398-05842-3

Library of Congress Catalog Card Number: 92-42964

Printed in the United States of America
SC-R-3

Library of Congress Cataloging-in-Publication Data

Megay-Nespoli, Karen.
 The first year for elementary school teachers : a practical plan
for dealing with the short and long-term management of teaching
duties and responsibilities / by Karen Megay-Nespoli.
  p. cm.
 Includes bibliographical references (p.) and index.
 ISBN 0-398-05842-3
 1. First year teachers—United States. 2. Elementary school
teachers—Training of—United States. 3. Classroom management—
United States. I. Title.
LB2844.1.N4M42 1993
372.11—dc20   92-42964
                    CIP

*This book is dedicated to my parents, Audrey and
Charles, who encouraged me to always "GO FOR IT!"
and
To my wonderful and supportive husband and family—
Michael, Lauren and Caitlin.*

ABOUT THE AUTHOR

Karen Megay-Nespoli has been an elementary school teacher for ten years. She received two Professional Diplomas from Saint John's University in the areas of Educational Leadership and Supervision and Administration. Mrs. Megay-Nespoli has worked in both public and parochial school systems. Her teaching experience has included working with gifted and talented, mainstreamed special education and non-English speaking students. She has been a cooperating teacher, having trained student teachers from several colleges.

Mrs. Megay-Nespoli performed the dual position of teacher and administrative assistant for four years, working extensively with beginning teachers.

She is married and the mother of two daughters. She is currently pursuing her Ed.D. in Gifted Education.

INTRODUCTION

Here you are straight out of college ready to meet your first class, armed with methods, manuals and guidelines to help you through the school year. You're excited, enthusiastic and eager to begin teaching. You're also a little bit nervous. You've got your teaching assignment and you're prepared. But you are about to find out that your college professors neglected to fill you in on some minor details. They neglected to teach you the finer points of your education—how to survive your first year of teaching.

This book was written to help you get through all the "firsts" in teaching. The things that the college professors spend little or no time explaining. For example, how to handle the first day of school and how to plan your first class trip.

These essential topics are rarely discussed except among new teachers and only when a problem occurs. You won't confide in an administrator for fear he'll think you're unqualified and you won't confide in a co-worker for fear they'll inform an administrator. Where do you go for help? Usually to another teacher who is new, like yourself, and going through the same problems. I know because that's what I did and together we muddled through the first year. We shared our triumphs and failures, and learned by trial and error.

When I became an administrator and worked with beginning teachers, I found that these new teachers were good teachers, but they were overwhelmed by all the "firsts" they had to face. It was beginning to affect their teaching. Together we came up with solutions to help them spend more time teaching and less time on non-teaching tasks.

I hope that this book will serve as a reference book for beginning teachers. I hope it will make your first year easier and help you to be a more confident and effective teacher.

You have the potential to be a really good teacher. The ONE some child will always remember. The ONE that can really make a difference. Welcome to teaching.

CONTENTS

THE FIRST YEAR FOR
ELEMENTARY SCHOOL TEACHERS

First Day of School

by Aileen Fisher

I wonder
    if my drawing
        will be as good as theirs.

I wonder
    if they'll like me
        or just be full of stares.

I wonder
    if my teacher
        will look like Mom or Gram.

I wonder
    if my puppy
        will wonder where I am.

Reprinted with permission of Aileen Fisher © 1962.

Chapter One

PREPARE YE

Welcome to:

    a. the first day of school.
    b. the first day of your new career.
    c. the first day of the rest of your life.
    d. all of the above.

If you selected choice a, b, c, or d you are correct. This is the moment you've waited for, well almost. Teachers begin the school year several days before the students arrive. We need this "quiet" time to organize and prepare the classroom. It is during these few days that you will begin to develop the confidence and assurance that will ensure a successful school year.

The days before school officially opens are hectic, but important. Your first day will probably begin with a faculty conference. At this conference you will meet your administrators, colleagues and receive essential information about your school and procedures. Information generally includes: class assignments, fire drill procedures, line up and dismissal times and procedures, contact personnel (who's in charge of what), information about supplies, books and materials, as well as information about your first day with the children. It is a good idea to take notes and write down any questions that you have. It is also a good idea to keep a folder with faculty conference notes for reference.

At this meeting you will have an opportunity to meet your colleagues and to make a friend or two. New teachers usually make friends with other new teachers, which is great for moral support, but also you should include someone who has been on the faculty who can show you the ropes, answer questions and help you grow as an educator.

During the next few days you will begin to organize your classroom, but first you should tour the school facility. Be sure to include: fire drill exits, lunch room facilities, school office, nurse's and guidance offices, faculty room, computer room, bathrooms, gym, auditorium and library. This tour will help you feel more "at home" and will let your students know that although you are new to the school, you are familiar with the facility.[1]

It may seem silly to tour the school, but it is not. We had a new teacher on staff who couldn't find her way to her own classroom. Every morning she would knock on my door and ask me to direct her to her classroom. It took her about two weeks before she could find it on her own. She also made the mistake of asking her students for directions to the gym—the children led her on a "wild goose chase." Needless to say this led to chaos and to her being reassigned to a new school.

Next you may want to preview your class records. Specifically: class lists, health cards, and cumulative record cards. In this preview you are looking for information about your students that will help you organize your classroom. For example, you need to know the number of students in your class so that you can obtain the correct number of desks. (I always ask for 2–3 extra desks for new admissions or transfer students.) The health records will help with a seating plan, those children with glasses, impairments or other handicaps may need special seating arrangements. It is also beneficial to be aware of any medical problems your students may have such as seizures or asthma attacks. By knowing your students and their needs you will make them more comfortable in their classroom.

I personally do not like to preview academic records until after I have met the children. I also dislike hearing about my students from their previous teacher. I like to believe that this is a new year, a new teacher and a new beginning for all of us. Once I've met the children and gotten to know them I go to my academic records to try to learn more about their strengths and weaknesses and where I must begin.

Previewing health records before school begins is very important. I had a situation occur with two boys who had the same first name. The health cards indicated that one of the boys was completely deaf in his left ear. Naturally I seated him in the front of the room where he could hear me and see me in case he needed to lip-read. He was doing beautifully the first few weeks of school, but the other boy was struggling and missing assignments. I noticed that when I moved around the room during a lesson this child could not follow the lesson. He couldn't hear me. The school nurse had both boys retested and we found a clerical error. The child's deafness had been recorded on the wrong child's record. Once the records and seating plan were corrected, both boys performed beautifully. The moral—read your records carefully and trust your instincts.

Preparing the classroom is a challenge not to be taken lightly. You want to create an atmosphere conducive to learning. You want it to be cheerful, but not distracting. You want your students to be comfortable there; after all it is their "home" for six hours a day.

Furniture placement should be your first priority. The desks, chairs, tables, cabinets and bookshelves can be moved to make the most of the space available. Begin slowly, be open and flexible to new ideas. As for help moving the heavier objects; get custodial help. Perhaps you can begin the school year with traditional straight rows. As you get to know your students and become more comfortable you can experiment. Keep in mind that you want the traffic of students to flow smoothly. You also do not want to block any fire exits.[2]

While you're moving the furniture around don't be surprised at what you may find: old books, chewing gum, pens, pencils or a mouse, yes a mouse. I was attempting to move a bookcase when, much to my surprise, I was greeted by a mouse. It was a fun school year, until they got the mice under control! So beware!

Next consider the placement of your desk. By placing your desk in front of the room, you may block valuable blackboard space, as well as hamper the children's visual access to the blackboard. By placing your desk in the back or side of the room you will be able to view everything, especially the children and the door. It will also force you to move away from your desk. You can't teach from behind a desk, mobility is important. By moving around the room you ensure that every child is on task and it allows you the opportunity to see everything that is happening in your classroom (figures 1 and 2). Mobility gives the teacher the opportunity to capture and hold the children's attention. It also helps build confidence and a warm relationship with your students.

After desk placement check the general appearance of your room. Check for broken windows, shades, closets, and locks. Make a list of necessary repairs and additional desks needed for the custodial staff. The custodial staff is an important part of the school plant. Get to know them; they are valued friends. I never had to take my plants home during winter or spring recess; the custodial staff was kind enough to water them for me.

Next take inventory of your classroom. Look for: an American flag, maps, globes, dictionaries, encyclopedias, reading and math kits, textbooks,

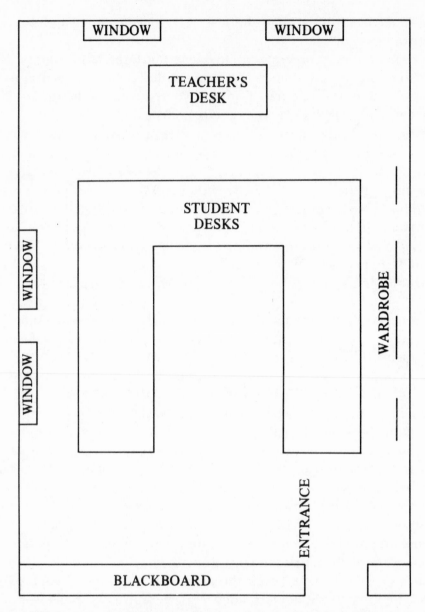

Figure 1. This is one way to arrange your classroom when you tire of the traditional rows. This U-shaped arrangement allows your students an optimal view of the blackboard.

class library, filmstrips, audio/visual equipment, and any other educational material that may be available. This list will help you to organize your classroom and will help you to develop Learning Centers at a later date.

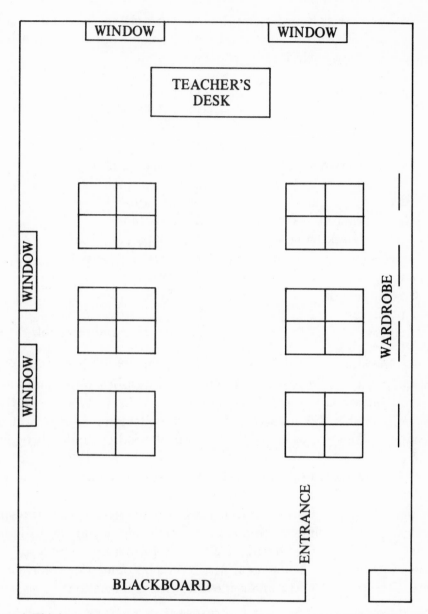

Figure 2. This is an alternative plan in which student desks are grouped. This works well with older students and for small group activities.

Bulletin boards are an integral part of every classroom. They should be decorative and reflective of the curriculum being taught. Check the appearance, location and number of bulletin boards in and outside your classroom. Begin to think about how you will utilize them.

Your next task is to order supplies for your classroom. Some schools give you a check off list, others ask you to create your own list. A basic supply list should include:

1. chalk/erasers
2. lined paper
3. construction paper
4. drawing paper
5. crayons/paints
6. scissors—1 pair teacher, several pairs for students
7. scotch/masking tape
8. stapler/staples/remover
9. red pens/pencils
10. pens/pencils
11. paper clips
12. rulers
14. plan book
15. file folders
16. note pads
17. writing paper
18. marking pens
19. hole punch
20. whistle
21. desk blotter
22. ink pad and stamps
23. reward stickers
24. yardstick
25. dictionary
26. clipboard
27. marking and roll book

Keep in mind that this is a basic list—a "no frills" list. It does not include: paint brushes, easels, bulletin board supplies, duplication masters or educational games. Most teachers purchase these items from a local Teacher's Store. Ask one of your colleagues to give you the directions. These stores contain a "wealth of goodies" and will be well worth the trip.

As you will soon find out, teaching is more than just working with children. It involves a great deal of paper work. The key is to stay on top of it and complete it before it is due. Many of the forms require the same information. If this information is easily accessible to you, your life will be simpler. Begin by gathering available information about your students and keep it in a notebook which will become your information guide. Each page should contain the following information:

1. Student's name
2. Student's identification number
3. Current address
4. Telephone number
5. Emergency number
6. Parent or Guardian's name
7. Birth date

All of this information can be found on the cumulative record card, except for the emergency telephone number which you can get from the emergency cards later on.[3]

It is also helpful to set up a simple filing system that is within reach. Folders for such things as: conference notes, school forms, permission slips, absence notes and parental correspondence are just a few that will help you to deal with all the paper work.

Last, but not least, you must prepare your lesson plans for the next two weeks. Keep them simple and focus on skills the children already have. The review will build their confidence and give you a good idea of where the children need some "brushing up."

In just a few days your students will be arriving so make the most of these quiet days. Remember June is only nine months away!

ENDNOTES

1. Dougherty, Anne: *Beginnings: A Guide for New Teachers.* Coronado, Beginnings, 1988, p. 21.
2. Rosen, Carol and Rudnick, Phyllis: *Teacher to Teacher.* New York, Harvin, 1987, pp. 1–3.
3. Meyers, Ellen. (Editor): *New Teachers Handbook.* New York, Impact II, 1988, p. 8.

Chapter Two

THAT ALL IMPORTANT FIRST DAY

That first day of school is perhaps the most important teaching day of the entire school year. You will be building the framework which will establish an excellent learning environment.

Your first task will be to meet and escort your class to their new classroom. Follow the procedure outlined at the faculty conference. If no procedure has been outlined, ask a colleague about the procedure prior to that first day.

It is a good idea to have the following information ready for inquiring parents: where and when the children will be dismissed for lunch and at the end of the school day. Try not to answer any questions you are not sure of. Tell the parent you will get back to them or refer them to the school office. First impressions do count, so be courteous to all parents. It's their first day too![1]

On the way to the classroom point out to your students the stairway being used. If they miss line up one morning they'll be able to find their way to the classroom.

Have your class enter the classroom and move toward the back; when everyone is inside, close your door. Seat the children one at a time, according to your pre-arranged seating plan. Alphabetical seating is usually best and do not forget about your visual or hearing impaired students.

Once the children are seated, introduce yourself. Write your name on the blackboard. Talk a little about yourself. Be enthusiastic and let them know you're happy to be there and to be their teacher.

Your next task will be to take attendance or call the roll. Make sure that everyone is present who should be in your class and give the office the names of those who are missing. Very often a child has transferred to a new school and the paper work hasn't been completed.

There are several types of information you want to express on that first day: information about classroom routines, exciting things to be learned and activities planned for the year.[2]

Classroom routines might include:

1. fire drill procedures
2. procedures for exiting and entering the room
3. where to store coats, jackets, book bags, and lunch boxes
4. procedures for using the lavatory and drinking fountains
5. what supplies will be needed
6. procedures for getting your attention

Exciting things to be learned:

1. spelling shortcuts
2. cursive writing
3. cinquain poetry
4. weather forecasting
5. object printing
6. simplifying fractions

Activities for the coming year:

1. Field trips—museum trips, movies, historical sights and other field day experiences
2. Art activities—calligraphy, collage, weaving, and block printing
3. Classroom games—sudden death, multiplication bingo, concentration and the match game

By now the children have been sitting while you've been doing all the talking. It is important to remember that these children have been active all summer and they're not ready to sit still. Be sure to plan some movement into your lesson plan. You can play Simon Says, use stretching exercises or teach a song which includes movement. This is a great activity to remember all year long. It really gets the blood flowing to their brains. The children are hesitant at first, they're not sure what you are up to, but they love it! I've even had the Principal come in and join us. We all need a break during the day, a change of pace—even teachers!

When they're settled back in their seats take a few minutes to acquaint them with their room. Point out the library corner, bulletin boards, reference books, learning centers, math and reading kits and any other materials you would like them to know about.

This is also a good time to discuss class rules. You can begin with a short discussion about rules and why they are necessary. Elicit rules from your students that they must obey outside the classroom. For example, waiting for the street light to turn green before crossing the street. Discuss why this is important and from there you can proceed to develop and discuss your class rules. Record these rules on a chart and keep them in plain sight. Your initial rule chart should be short—about 5–6 rules. New rules can be added as they are necessary.

Again another movement activity will help. This time you can take a walking tour of the school building. This is particularly important with younger children, but works just as well with older children. I found the older children are curious to see if everything is the same as they left it. You may want to include the following, depending on the age group: lavatory, lunch room, basement, library, computer lab, nurse's and guidance offices as well as the main office.

With these preliminaries over you are ready to teach your class. The teacher who comes to school on the very first day with prepared lessons will have a successful school year. You can begin with several Welcome Back Activities. Some activity ideas may include:[3]

THIS IS ME—A fun way to describe themselves. Have each child write their name vertically on the left side of the paper. The children then write an adjective to describe themselves using the letters of their name.

S —Sweet	B —Brilliant
U —Understanding	R —Rascal
S —Silly	I —Intelligent
A —Artistic	A —Adorable
N —Neat	N —Nice

The children may use a dictionary or a thesaurus for help. You can really learn a great deal about a child and how they view themselves with this activity.

BREAK THE CODE—Have photocopied sheets on which the first and last names of ten Disney or nursery rhyme characters are written in code. Each child is given a copy and asked to break the code. The first child to complete all ten successfully can be the teacher and check other student's work or lend assistance.

19 14 15 23   23 8 9 24 5   = SNOW WHITE

$$\overline{10\ 1\ 3\ 11} \quad \overline{1\ 14\ 4} \quad \overline{10\ 9\ 12\ 12} = \text{JACK AND JILL}$$

HELPING HANDS — Have the children trace both of their hands, cut them out and decorate them. You can now create a mini math lesson.

1. How many children are there? How many hands? How many fingers?
2. If we only use one hand for each child, how many hands will we have? How many fingers?
3. If we subtract all the boys' hands from the class, how many will we have? If we subtract the girls' hands?

Please be careful when using this lesson. Often there are students who have missing fingers or their hands are deformed. In this case it is best to skip this activity.

Now have your students put their name on each of their decorated hands and collect them. You can use these hands to assign class jobs. List the job and place the hand of the child who is responsible for that job next to it.

You can also use the hands to decorate your Bulletin Boards. They can be used as a decorative border or use the hands to spell the subject areas.

NAME TAGS — For younger children you might want to supply them with paper and crayons to create a name tag. You could then discuss the colors they used and how each color makes them feel. You can discuss favorite colors and count how many different colors were used.

STORIES — This is great for younger children, but, surprisingly, enough older children enjoy this activity also.

Picture books are great for younger children. Sesame Street books provide many interesting topics for young readers. Third and fourth graders love the Amelia Bedelia series and older children enjoy reading mystery books such as the Cam Jansen series. I've even used *Tales of the Arabian Knights, The Adventures of Tom Sawyer* and *The Knights of the Round Table.* If you read them a chapter each day you leave them wanting more!

Try to keep your activities simple, use activities and formats with a whole group focus or those which require simple procedures. By keeping the tasks simple you will promote a high rate of success and your students will begin to feel more comfortable with their new class and teacher.

Somewhere during these activities the lunch bell will ring and you will have an opportunity to regroup. It is important that you eat lunch, you need your strength, you need to keep your body healthy. It is also an excellent opportunity to work on new friendships with your colleagues. You can share some memorable moments from your first day.

The afternoon will give you a chance to try out some more of your lessons and maybe even try a game or a song with your class.

Toward the end of the school day it will be time to get things ready to go home to the parents. This is a good time to establish a procedure for bringing school information home. Each child can create an information folder where school notices are kept and taken home at the end of the day. This will help parents too. They will know where to look for information rather than scrambling around the bottom of the school bag for crumpled notes.

The parent information folder would include:

- school calendar, information and forms for school collection of milk money, banking, and other informational forms.
- school procedures—required notes for absence, early dismissal procedures for dental or doctor appointments.
- class routines—a note from the teacher explaining class routines, homework requirements, supply list, testing schedule (every Friday Spelling and Math test) and need for parent volunteers.

By this time your energy level will be waning, but hang in there, the day is almost over. End the day on a positive note. Tell them how beautifully the day went. How well they participated in the activities you planned. How well they all got along with each other. What good listeners they were and how you enjoyed working with them.

Don't forget to save a little energy for the parents who will be waiting to speak to you as you dismiss your class. A smile and a kind word can go a long way.[4]

If you are apprehensive about your first day, you are not alone. I can remember my knees knocking as I left the house that morning. There's nothing more terrifying, nor exciting as your "first day." There will always be good days and bad days—here's to a year of great days!

BEYOND THE FIRST DAY

Congratulations, you made it through the first day. Do you wonder what the rest of the week will be like? More of the same. Some new faces (students), interruptions, schedule changes and lots of paper work. Unfortunately, textbooks are rarely delivered until the end of the first week and sometimes even later. You must have your own materials and you must overplan. Don't be caught short. Keep the lessons simple which will allow the children to meet with success. They are nervous and eager to show you what they know. Meeting with success early in the school year will encourage them to learn more and become comfortable in participating in your lessons for the rest of the school year.

You can use this time to study your new class. You can really get acquainted with your new class, by just observing them in this learning environment. If you know what to look for when studying children, you can better help these children adapt to their new learning environment.

Here are some things to look for when studying children:

1. Manner of entering the classroom and taking a seat
2. General social classroom atmosphere
3. General grooming for individuals
4. Promptness in coming to attention
5. Attitude toward the teacher
6. Types of pupil responses
7. Speech and language problems
8. Specific behavior displayed in attempts to gain peer or teacher approval
9. Extent of class participation
10. Tendencies to dominate discussions
11. Tendency to become involved in irrelevant activities
12. Nature and extent of interest in learning
13. Care in which assignments have been prepared
14. Types of questions asked by students
15. Ability levels of individual student's work and study habits
16. Attempts at cheating or other forms of dishonesty
17. Physical appearance—cuts, bruises and other observable markings
18. Attitudes toward classmates
19. Extreme shyness and reticence to participate in activities
20. Other inappropriate behaviors.[5]

You won't notice all of these behaviors in every child, but as the children become more comfortable several of these behaviors may emerge. They can be the early warning signs of learning or behavior problems, child abuse or giftedness. Yes, very often gifted children act out due to boredom so don't rule giftedness out!

Keep a small notebook in which you can jot down a few lines when you notice an inappropriate behavior. It is important to note the date, time and circumstances that led to the specific behavior. Sometimes it is the circumstances that caused the behavior and sometimes it is the time of day. For example, the children seem to have the most energy after lunch and this often leads to trouble. They don't know how to channel that energy.

Having the facts together in a notebook allows you to have these facts on hand when you are discussing the child with parents, supervisors or educational and psychological evaluators.

Remember, too, that not all behaviors are bad. I had a student who loved to "doodle." He had great artistic ability. We struck a deal—he could "doodle" when his work was completed and correct. I supplied him with paper and various types of art supplies and he was thrilled. His grades improved and he got to "doodle" too. He designed all of our scenery for our class play and was in charge of designing all the programs for the various school events. Years later I wrote a letter of recommendation for him to attend a special art school.

Another child was constantly showing off, calling out, seeking approval from both peers and teacher. He was having trouble dealing with his giftedness. He didn't want to be smart, he wanted to be accepted by his peers. We talked about ways to seek approval, make friends and utilize his giftedness.

Other cases were not as pleasant. A child with poor grooming habits was a victim of child neglect. Due to family problems no one was taking care of him. No one saw that he bathed nor did they launder his clothes. Sometimes he did not even have lunch. After several meetings with his family, we had to alert the authorities and the situation did improve.

Last, the story of the class "Bully" and tough guy. He threatened children all the time, but never really followed through. He was covering his inability to read. He was terrific at math, but couldn't read. He was the perfect student during the math lesson, but acted out constantly during reading. He received extra help outside the classroom as well as in class. His teacher used his strength in math to help him read. Needless to say the "Bully" calmed down considerably and learned how to read too!

You can see from these examples that studying students can certainly pay off. It is to your advantage to identify problems—big or small. Not only are you helping that one child, you are helping the class and yourself. Fewer learning and behavior problem leave more time for learning, which is why you became a teacher in the first place!

Parent Night

Some time in September or early October, you will be asked to participate in Parent's Night. The evening begins with a general meeting for all parents and teachers. At this meeting the Principal welcomes the parents and tells them about the school, rules, procedures and staff. The Principal may also ask some key faculty members to say a few words. At this time the Parent-Teachers Association (P.T.A.) President may take the floor and talk about the P.T.A. and urge the parents to become active members. After the general meeting the parents are invited to their child's classroom to meet the teacher.

This is your "big moment," use it to your advantage. You have all the parents gathered in your room. What do you want them to know about you, the way you run your classroom, the curriculum you will cover this year and their role in their child's education. Your presentation should take no more than fifteen to twenty minutes, so make them count.

Here are some tips:

1. On several 3 by 5 index cards, make yourself an outline of everything you'd like the parents to know:
   a. curriculum and textbooks
   b. reading program
   c. routines, procedures and rules
   d. parental role in their child's education
2. Put an asterisk next to the important items. If your presentation is running long, you can just cover the important items.
3. Practice what you are going to say, rather than relying heavily on the index cards.
4. Move around the room, as you would during a lesson. Point out the bulletin boards, library corner and learning centers.
5. Leave some time for parent questions. Let them know you

are available to speak to them individually by appointment and are eager to keep the lines of communication open.

6. When you are through be sure to thank the parents for coming.

Other helpful hints:

1. Place a Welcome sign on your door with your name and class number. This will help parents to find your room quickly.
2. Make sure the room is clean and that student work is displayed prominently.
3. Dress comfortable and professionally. First impressions do count.
4. Write your name on the blackboard.
5. Have a sign-in sheet for the parents. You will then know which parents were unable to attend and will not be familiar with your policies.
6. Keep all your notes in a file for next year. With a few minor changes you'll be ready for the next Parent Night.

ENDNOTES

1. Rosen, Carol and Rudnick, Phyllis: *Teacher to Teacher.* New York, Harvin, 1987, p. 9.
2. Tingey-Michaelis, Carol: "Day One! How to Handle that All Important First Day." *Early Years, 15:* 37–38, 1984.
3. Flynn, Jean: *Preparation for the First Day,* Chicago, Continental Press, 1973, pp. 7–10.
4. Tingey-Michaelis, op. cit., p. 38.
5. Brown, Susan: "What to Look for When Studying Children." Media Workshop, 1971, p. 5.

Chapter Three

EFFECTIVE CLASSROOM MANAGEMENT

WANTED: EFFECTIVE CLASSROOM MANAGER

Must have the ability to recognize, interpret and respond to the events that occur daily within the classroom. Must be able to organize your time, classroom space, materials and students to create a positive learning environment.

Would you answer this want ad? By selecting teaching as a career, you've already answered this ad. Effective teachers are good classroom managers. Without good management skills, little or no learning will take place in your classroom.

Don't panic—a management course is not necessary, but you may want to brush up on a few behavior patterns associated with more effective classroom management. Kounin identified the following behaviors:

With-it-ness is a teacher's ability to communicate to her students that she knows what they are doing in the classroom at all times (in other words, having eyes in the back of your head!). The easiest way for teachers to let their students know they are "with-it" is to constantly monitor classroom behavior and nip behavior problems in the bud before they escalate. I find that by moving around the classroom, I'm able to see and stop inappropriate behavior before it becomes a problem. It also keeps my students on their toes—they never quite know where I'll be next!

Overlapping is described as the teacher's ability to effectively handle any classroom situation while teaching a lesson at the same time. A typical situation might be a student returning from a pull-out program while you are teaching a math lesson; or teaching a lesson and dealing with a student's misbehavior. You must maintain the flow of your lesson while at the same time dealing with the interruption. In situation one, a "buddy" student could help the returning child until you have a moment for that child. In situation two, I would continue my lesson while moving toward the misbehavior which usually stops without a word from the teacher. The key is to keep your lesson going, no matter what the interruption. There will be times when this does not work. When a fellow teacher enters the room or the public address system is being used. For these times you need to establish a procedure so your students will know what to do.

Momentum is the ability to keep a steady flow throughout your lesson and throughout the school day. It is best to set a brisk pace, moving from one activity to the next and from one lesson to the next. Avoid lecturing and lengthy explanations. Break your lessons down into small activities, this will move your lesson along at a steady pace. Keeping a brisk pace will keep the students actively engaged in learning.

Smoothness is the teacher's ability to move smoothly from one lesson or learning activity to another. The key here is to use routines, cues and signals to prepare your students for the transition. Some teachers use an agenda listed on the blackboard. This cues the students to the next activity. Verbally you can tell your students to close their books, clear their desks or take out a notebook. Assigning students to give out supplies, books or collect materials often eliminates potential problems. Whatever procedure you adopt will help to make a smooth transition.

Group Focus or "time on task" refers to a teacher's ability to keep the students actively engaged in that learning activity. Structure the activities so that all students are actively participating. This can be accomplished by having students read aloud, answer questions, write on the blackboard, holding students accountable for doing their work and by creating suspenseful and high interest lessons. Teachers often forget to use audio-visual aids such as: overhead projectors, slides, video tapes, or filmstrips. Just setting up the equipment creates student interest. I also use the blackboard as a teaching tool by creating "fill in the blank" or matching exercises. The children love to come up to the blackboard.[1]

Don't worry about mastering all of these behaviors at once or even by the first day of school. It takes time and practice especially getting use to those "eyes in back of your head."

There are several teacher practices that you can begin to use immediately. A good classroom arrangement is the best place to begin because it eliminates potential distractions for students and minimizes opportunities for students to disrupt others.

Begin by arranging students' seats so students can easily see the blackboard and other instructional displays. A good classroom arrange-

ment permits an easy flow of traffic throughout the room. Avoid conges-
tion in high traffic areas such as at the pencil sharpener, storage areas,
bookshelves, learning centers and exits, by facilitating ready access to
these areas. Your arrangement should also ensure high visibility so you
can quickly and easily monitor students in all areas of the room. Sounds
like a tall order, but it really isn't. Draw a few arrangements yourself.
Check the points mentioned above, then move your furniture. (Be on the
look out for that mouse!) It's easier to draw first and move second. Ask
the custodian to help with the heavier items. Keep all of your drawings
for the future; by mid-semester you'll be looking for a change.

The next step is to plan how you want your classroom to operate and to
develop a set of rules and procedures to meet your goals. Our primary
goal as educators is to help children develop positive attitudes, to encourage other children and adults to enjoy learning experiences. This confidence enables children to become curious, creative, and independent
achievers. Let's begin with rules.

Rules should govern student behavior such as student talking, respect
for others and their property. Limit the number of rules. Five or six
positive ones are sufficient. Design rules the students understand and
which will encourage them to take responsibility for their behavior. Print
and display these rules for your students.

Procedures apply to specific instructional routines or housekeeping
tasks. You should identify the desired behavior for each area and stipu-
late the procedure you intend to use.

Here are some procedures you may want to include:

1. Beginning the school day—Taking seats, going to the coat closet,
   attendance, collections and passing back graded papers.
2. Interruptions—Establish procedures for meeting interruptions such
   as the Public Address System or another teacher entering the
   room.
3. Fire Drill—These routines should be simple and direct and their
   importance understood.
4. Group Activities (reading groups)—Children should know how to
   move from group to group, how to return to their seats, what
   materials to take with them, what behavior is expected of them in
   the group and the behavior of those not in the group.
5. Student participation—Should students raise their hands or speak
   in turn and how should they treat the speaker?

6. Assignments—Where are they posted? When should they be copied into their assignment pads? How should they be done?
7. Behavior during seat work—Should students be totally silent? Should they raise their hands for help? Does this behavior change when they work in small groups?
8. What to do when work is through—Make a chart with several options—sit quietly, check over your work, study, read, do extra credit work or free time activity.
9. Turning in assignments—When should they be turned in? Where should they be placed—folder, desk, box, shelves or other designated area?
10. Make-up work—Procedures for helping absent students make up assignments missed and procedures for communicating these assignments to students.
11. Out of seat—When is it acceptable and when does a student need permission? (I had one standing rule—if you were nauseous and about to vomit, do not ask permission, run for the bathroom!)
12. Passing out books and materials—Procedures on what to do while waiting, who will distribute materials and where to put materials that are returned? (I assigned monitors on a monthly basis to distribute and collect materials—this eliminates numerous children volunteering all at once.)
13. Use of classroom materials—Desks, book shelves, cabinets, and teacher's desk. Who has access and under what conditions?
14. Specific routines and procedures—Needed for the bathroom, playground and lunchroom.[2]

Once you've developed a set of rules and procedures they should be taught to your students as you would any other content area. This involves:

1. Presenting rules and procedures as they are needed by students, rather than inundating them with rules and procedures on day one.
2. Carefully explain each rule or procedure and where possible demonstrate the behavior yourself or have several students demonstrate the desired behavior.
3. Provide a discussion session for the students as to why rules and procedures are necessary. As young as kindergarten, children

know why there are rules. You can talk about traffic rules, it usually sparks an interesting discussion. If the children are older, you may want your students to help you develop the rules—students are more likely to follow rules they have developed rather than rules that were forced upon them. The choice is yours.

4. Review and re-teach rules and procedures as necessary and provide feedback to your students. Let them know when these rules and procedures are working or not working. Re-evaluate these rules and procedures in the event that these rules and procedures do not work with this year's class.

Effective managers also develop a reasonable system for consistently reinforcing their rules and procedures which includes positive feedback and rewards for good behavior and fair and appropriate consequences for inappropriate behavior.

Don't make the mistake I made during my first year. My idea of punishment was a writing exercise, mostly consisting of spelling words ten times each, times tables five times each and copying the dictionary. My desk was full of "punishment exercises" and the problems were still there. A fact—my writing assignments were easier than doing class work assignments so it encouraged misbehavior. The children gained nothing by writing useless exercises and I had a desk full of paper. I still believe in writing assignments, but now they are more personal. I select an assignment for each child based on their area of weakness. For example, if a student's area of weakness is reading comprehension, they are assigned a few reading comprehension exercises. If it is long division, then they must complete several long division problems. Now they learn two valuable lessons—don't break the rules and how to "bone up" on academics.

Before you resort to writing assignments, you need to establish a hierarchy of consequences. These consequences may range from:

1. Establishing eye contact or moving closer to the student.
2. Have the student re-state the broken rule, have a private talk with the student, withhold a privilege or give an appropriate assignment.
3. Contact the parents and work with them, develop a behavior contract or meet with the child, parents and Principal to discuss the problem.

Your students should be aware of these sanctions. They can be introduced and discussed after you have presented your class rules.[3] If there are repeated incidents, note the date, time, what happened and the circumstances in your anecdotal notebook. Often there is a pattern to the behavior. Some children find it difficult to settle down after lunch or after missing the school bus. Your anecdotal record of these events will help you to see if there is a pattern. After each inappropriate behavior, remind the student of the next sanction and note it in your record. This will also come to be a valuable tool when talking to the parents. You not only have the exact information at your fingertips, but often parents will tell you about something that happened at home which may have provoked that "inappropriate behavior" which may help in handling that problem.

Children do not automatically know what constitutes appropriate behavior. They have to be taught, that is why I have stressed teaching, reteaching and restating the broken rule. Discipline should be teaching appropriate forms of behavior, rather than a series of punishments. Instead of removing the child from the learning situation, we should stop the inappropriate behavior, coach an alternative behavior and send the child back into the situation to practice the new behavior. Once children know that we are helping them find new ways of accomplishing what they want to do, they will begin to think out more acceptable ways themselves.[4] (I would not suggest using this method with older students or in a hostile situation where it may embarrass the child. It is appropriate for young children who are in the primary grades, which is the perfect place to teach appropriate behavior.)

One last word on classroom management. Children learn by example. When we teach safety, voice control, ways to deal with anger and care of materials we need to model these behaviors ourselves. We must show the same respect and concern for a child that we show to adults. Children, like adults, are far from perfect and will occasionally come to school not feeling well, in a grumpy mood, with problems from home, missing the school bus and a host of other situations that can cause less than perfect behavior. We need to do our best to understand that children are people too and they're entitled to an "off day" now and again.

Successful classroom management is the key to learning. Students learn best when they know what is expected of them and when the organizational and instructional skills are appropriately matched with their learning needs and styles. You now have the means to build a strong foundation for good classroom management. Go out there and make it happen!

ENDNOTES

1. Kounin, Jacob: *Discipline and Group Management in Classrooms.* New York, Holt, 1970.
2. Megay-Nespoli, Karen: "Effective Classroom Management." *Today's Catholic Educator 17:* 1984 p. 37.
3. Rauth, Marilyn: "Research on Effective Classroom Management for the Beginning of the School Year." Washington, D.C., *AFT.* 1985. p. 15.
4. Clewett, Anne S. "Discipline as Teaching, Rather than Punishment." *Young Children XLIII* 1988. pp. 26–31.

Chapter Four

PLAN, PLAN, PLAN

Aim: To understand the purpose of a curriculum and curriculum guide.

To learn how these materials can help make lesson planning easier.

Motivation: On your first day as a new teacher you are given seven or eight curriculum guides and five or six textbooks. What will you do with these materials? Where do you begin?

Lesson: Selecting your first plan book is a momentous occasion. There are so many to choose from. My first plan book was royal blue, and written in gold lettering were the words, PLAN BOOK. What impressed me about this book was the size of the preprinted boxes. I needed plenty of room to write my lesson plans. What I didn't fully understand was the preplanning that takes place before you write the lesson plans and how helpful a curriculum guide can be.

A curriculum is a plan of study for a given subject at a specific grade level. It embodies all the information that scholars, administrators and teachers believe is essential to a literate, educated citizen.

A curriculum guide itemizes this plan of study into: goals, objectives, skills, content and activities to be taught.[1] Simply, a curriculum guide tells you what you need to teach.

When you are presented with several curriculum guides and textbooks, what do you do first? Find a comfortable chair and read through one guide. Reading through the guide gives you the entire picture—where to start, where to go and where to end. As you are reading, outline the essential skills to be covered.

Next go through the textbook and list the skills that are presented in the curriculum guide, but not in your textbook. You will need to decide how you will incorporate the skills that are not present in the textbook. Then list the skills that are taught in the text, but not in your curriculum guide. You will need to decide if these skills will be included in your goals or if you will use them for enrichment material?[2]

The outline you have created can now become your teaching goals for the school year.

Homework: Using your goals and textbook, estimate the length of time you think you will need to teach each unit. This is only an estimate; some units may take several weeks and others only a week or two.

Follow Up: Ask your mentor or another veteran teacher to review your goals and time schedule. An experienced teacher can often suggest which skills will require more or less time. They also know which skills are tested more frequently. A mentor can help make planning easier and more effective.

Once you have completed your goals and time schedules for each subject, you are ready to write lesson plans.

Summary: A curriculum and curriculum guide are tools to help you educate your students. They tell you what to teach; how you teach those skills is up to you. Be creative, experiment and use the guide as a springboard for your own ideas. Keep your goals and schedules handy. Make notes on which skills needed more or less time. These notes will save you even more time next year. (Providing you are teaching the same grade, the state hasn't revised the curriculum or the textbook hasn't changed!)

LESSON PLANS

Or What to do After the Bell Rings!

No doubt by now you have written several brilliant lesson plans for your college courses. Now comes the hard part, writing effective lesson plans for your class. Here's a quick review:

Lesson plans come in all sizes, shapes and forms. They can be written in preprinted lesson plan books, a spiral notebook or a loose-leaf binder. Whatever, you select as your personal choice, keep it neat and legible; others will be reading your plans. Who are these others? Your supervisor, principal or mentor will be checking or using your plan book from time to time. For the most part this is your book and your plans.

There is no perfect format for writing a lesson plan. You may want to check with your supervisor as to the format they prefer you to use. All forms have the same basic components: a beginning, middle and end.

A lesson plan begins with a purpose, objective or aim. You must decide what the student needs to learn. It can be a process, such as addition of whole numbers or sharing information like George Washington, the Father of Our Country. Your aim can be a simple statement or it can be a question. Once you've decided the aim of your lesson, you need to show your students why they need to learn this material. This is called the motivation part of your lesson plan and it is an important part of your lesson. Many students fail to achieve to their full potential because they lack the motivation to learn.

How can you motivate students to learn? Dr. P. Anderson and Dr. L. Laminack suggest these motivational techniques:

Infuse your students with curiosity. Children are naturally curious and an insightful teacher will tap into this curiosity. You can do this by bringing in something relevant to the topic. It can be as simple as a picture, a book, a plant or some souvenir you've collected. You will be surprised as to the kinds of questions your students will ask.

Make materials meaningful to students' lives and future goals. You can impel your students to master basic skills as the foundation for later success and by eliciting careers the students might select. Then match curriculum skills necessary for those careers. You may want to invite business people from the community to discuss their careers or invite a few parents to share their careers with the class.

Show interest and enthusiasm for the topic. When a teacher enters the room dressed as Abraham Lincoln, spouting the Gettysburg Address, you may get a laugh, but you've also got their attention. A bulletin board covered with palm trees, paper leis, pictures of hula girls and soft island music is a great way to introduce the Hawaiian Islands. By modeling enthusiasm or creating an atmosphere for learning you've motivated your students.

Involve your students through the use of discussion, discovery approaches, individual assignments and group planning. Before beginning a topic find out what they would like to learn about that topic. Without giving answers, you have set the stage for putting your students in charge of their own learning tasks. Have the children answer their own questions through interviews, research, presentations, or field trips. You'll be pleasantly surprised.

Introduce your class to alternatives to traditional formats. Everyone hates to write a book report. Let them explore alternative forms; murals, riddles, oral reports, crossword puzzles or character sketches. I've received a book report on cassette tape, video tape and even a computerized book report. Choices motivate learning.

Vary the types of activities your students will be doing. The way to keep your classroom fresh and exciting is to be creative. Possible activities could include: role playing, task slips, changing seats, reading aloud, watching a filmstrip, listening to an audio tape, brainstorming, team learning, or video taping a project.[3]

Once your students are motivated it is time to present your lesson. This can be done in a number of ways. Talking, lecturing, questioning, reading, games, audio-visual presentations and demonstrating are a few examples of teaching strategies. When you are deciding which strategies to use, use several, the more the better. People of all abilities learn in different ways. Your students are no exception. The more strategies you incorporate, the more learning styles you will recognize.

Claudia E. Cornett suggests the following strategies to meet the variety of learning styles found in your classroom.

1. Use questions of all types to stimulate various levels of thinking.
2. Provide a general overview of material to be learned so that students' past experiences will be associated with new ideas.
3. Allow sufficient time for information to be processed and then integrated.
4. Expect that at least one new thing will be learned by each student. Have your students share what they have learned once each day. This will encourage them to learn something new each day.
5. Set a clear purpose to each experience. What are they to listen for, read for or look for?
6. Use brainstorming to get your students warmed up before a lesson. You'll find out what they already know about the topic.
7. Teach visual mnemonics whenever you can. How many of us know the colors of the rainbow thanks to Roy G. Biv?
8. Use a multisensory approach in your lesson. That is, give directions orally, as well as visually. I usually do this with homework assignments. I write the assignment, then give it orally.
9. Use a variety of summary techniques: role playing, reciting, or creative writing can bring closure to learning.
10. Use descriptive feedback. "Each problem you've completed so far is correct." "I like the way you described how you felt when the dog bit you."[4]

You probably won't be able to master all these strategies in a week, but do try them, experiment and incorporate them into your lessons.

End your lesson with a brief summary, followed by a question period. I tried to impress upon my students to ask questions in class. It's too late when they are home trying to do their homework or taking the unit test. If they don't have any questions give a few reinforcement questions of your own. Use a sample question from their homework assignment. This is a good indication if your students have learned what you had hoped. You can also provide an activity to review or reinforce the new skill, such as a blackboard game or worksheet. Don't forget their homework assignment to further reinforce the skill.

Your lesson plans should cover no less than two weeks' work. Planning biweekly is easier and less nerve-wracking. While planning take into account testing days, holidays, assembly programs and other interruptions which might upset instructional time. Also consider the timing of major projects and tests. If you schedule these together they'll be due at the same time and you'll begin to feel the stress of grading. Keep in mind your personal obligations as well. Staggering the dates will reduce stress.[5]

It is best to plan for more than you will probably accomplish. Over-planning is far better than having nothing planned. Always plan a "little something extra" to fill in should you need it. Music activities, art projects, math games or spelling bees are great fillers, but planning an enrichment activity is much more rewarding.

Periodically assess your lesson planning. I'm sure your supervisor and mentor teacher will comment and help you to develop better plans. Use this feedback and your own feelings to evaluate your lesson planning. Write yourself notes indicating successes and failures and changes to make next time. Write them in your plan book. Refer to these notes for future planning. This not only will save you time, but will save you from repeating the same mistakes.

Lesson plans reflect what material you intend to cover. Be flexible in your planning. Don't rush, if you need more time on a certain topic, take it. You can make up the time some time later. It may become frustrating at times. You will feel as if you are falling behind and your students are not learning. Remember too that you are also learning—how to be organized and yet be flexible. It is a difficult balance, but somehow you'll learn to manage it all.

HOMEWORK

What is the purpose of giving homework assignments to your students?

A. To reinforce what the children are learning in the classroom.
B. To establish good work habits, independence and self-discipline.
C. Choice A and B. It is up to the individual teacher.[6]

The correct answer is the letter C. The individual teacher must decide the purpose of the homework assignment, before they can begin to plan the assignment.

If you wish to reinforce classroom learning you can assign drill and practice exercises. These can be found in workbooks, textbooks, worksheets and in the teacher's edition of most textbooks.

If your purpose is to establish good work habits, your assignments can be more creative. For example, I assigned each child in my class a different state in the United States. Each child was given a report guide to help them with the assignment. The guide helps the children to organize their materials, and helps them select research materials for their report. The entire assignment is a learning experience from how to use the library, how to select research material, and how to write the report.

Your students will need to be taught how to do their homework. Do not take it for granted that by fourth grade they know how to complete their homework. They don't—at least not to your specifications. I usually wait a day or two into the school year before I discuss homework. You will teach them how to do their homework as if it were any other subject. You will review the procedures often for optimal results.

The first thing you need is a homework policy. Let your students know the value of homework, why you assign homework, how you would like it completed and what role, if any, parental support will play. (Do you want parents to correct the child's homework or initial the assignment to indicate it is completed?) Next describe the consequences for not completing assignments. Will you grade their homework, if so what percent of their grade will be affected? Make sure your students understand your homework policy. You may want to put it in writing and have it hang prominently in your classroom as a constant reminder.

You may also want to discuss what they can do at home to assure their assignments are completed properly. I call this lesson "Good Study Habits or How to Keep the Dog from Eating your Homework." We talk about a study place: a well lighted room, no television, or radio just a quiet place to study. Then we talk about homework supplies: desk or table, pens, paper, pencils, erasers, etc. I ask them to set a specific time each day to do their homework and to keep them in a folder with their books so they won't be left behind.

To help make homework assignments more meaningful, why not try these suggestions:

1. Set aside time every day to check and review homework assignments.
2. Consistently praise and comment positively on the assignment. Put it in writing in addition to verbal praise. Comments are great motivators.
3. A homework bulletin board will show your students the importance you put on homework assignments. You can call it "Hurray for Homework!" The children love a chance to show off.[7]

The mere mention of the word "Homework" scares most children and adults alike. Homework can be fun with just a little help from you.

As you can tell, planning is a huge part of your job as a teacher. It involves a great deal of time and energy. As a new teacher you will probably spend more time planning than you will teaching. At times, it will seem overwhelming. Try to keep in mind that the results of your planning will yield more effective and organized teaching. By year's end you will enjoy a real sense of accomplishment.

Sample Outline of Goals

Mathematics Curriculum—Grade 4

I. Multiplication of whole numbers

basic facts
multiplication by zero; by one
commutative property of multiplication
multiples of a number
multiplication of 2 and 3 place numbers
multiplication of 3 digits by 2 digits with
exchange in any column

Estimate: 4 weeks beginning in January

II. Division of whole numbers

basic facts
role of one as divisor, zero as dividend

recording and reading division symbols
inverse operations
concept of repeated division
division of up to 4 digit numbers by 10 and multiples of ten
division of a 4 digit number by a two digit number

Estimate: 6 weeks beginning February into March

Sample Lesson Plan

April 29, 199__

Science 3

Aim: To show that different colors absorb heat at different rates.

Materials: 4–5 identical glasses
4–5 rubber bands
4–5 different colors of construction paper
1 pair of scissors
4–5 identical thermometers

Motivation:

Show the various colors of construction paper to the class. Ask: Which colors do you think will heat up faster?

Lesson:

Write the responses to your question on the blackboard. Fill the glasses to the same level, put a thermometer in each glass. Let them sit until equalized. Record temperature. Wrap a different colored piece of construction paper around each glass and secure with a rubber band. One glass should be left uncovered, make one white and one black. Let class decide on other colors. Put glasses in a sunny window.

Observe and record temperatures at 1/2 hour intervals. Water in the glasses with darker paper should heat up faster.

Reinforcement:

Have your class record readings in their science notebooks.

Homework:

Present these scientific findings on a line graph, or write a scientific report explaining the findings of this study.

Follow Up:

How do these findings affect the way we dress in the summer and in the winter?

GRADE OR CLASS __Sample Plan Book Page__

Math	Language Arts / Spelling	Reading	Groups
MONDAY — Numeration Aim: Review add. facts with sums to 18. Use txtbk p. 20+21 even #s only Vocab. addition, addend sum Hmwk p. 21 1-30 odd #s only	Words with short u Aim: To introduce 20 spelling words with short u. Pretest, Review + Correct WKBK p. 14 HMWK - Write each word 4x	Rhymes + Reasons Aim: Using context clues to understand multiple meanings. TRINA + MAGGIE p. 36-46 Voc. dev. Context clues oral reading Comprehension questions from T.E.	Full Circle Aim: Predicting the outcome of a story. THE JAPANESE ROOSTER p 34-44 Seatwork p. 9-12 Main Idea p. 3-5 Voc. Review p. 12-13
TUESDAY — Aim: Finding the sum of two numbers where order does not affect the sum. Use # cards + students to demonstrate. Use txtbk p. 22 + 23 Review + ck. Hmwk p 331 Set #11	Aim: Practice using short u words. Divide class into teams of 2 to work on a cloze story WKBK p. 15 HMWK - Using 10 spelling words write your own cloze story.	Aim: Using context clues to understand new vocabulary words. GROWING UP IN AMERICA 47-49 Seatwork 8-11 Context clues 4-8 Vocab. review 11-12	Aim: Improving Comprehension skills PEANUTS FOR SALE 44-47 Voc. dev. Comprehension skill Oral reading Review seatwork
WEDNESDAY — Aim: Adding ones + tens to ones using basic facts + patterns. Demonstrate with # line Read p. 24 complete p 25 in teams of 2. review + ck. Hmwk p. 331 Set #12	Aim: What is a suffix? How does it change word meanings? Demonstrate using word addition cards. Then do txbk Ch 2 p 22-24. Review cloze stories. Hmwk - Use 10 spelling words to create a puzzle.	Aim: Understanding and using vocabulary appropriately. GROWING UP IN AMERICA 47-49 Voc. dev. Oral reading Comprehension check Review previous wk	Aim: Understanding a reading selection. A BOX FOR MR. ABE 48-52 Seatwork 13-16 Main Idea 6-9 Voc. review 14-16
THURSDAY — Aim: Learning to find sums by grouping addends. Intro. Commutative + Associate Laws Read p. 26 Use txtbk p 27 odd #s only Hmwk p. 27 even #s only	Aim: More work with short u spelling words. Use cloze stories + spelling puzzles to review words. Post test Hmwk - WKBK p. 17 Study for test.	Aim: To strengthen skills. SRA Reading Individualized Program	all reading Kit Reading
FRIDAY — Aim: Solving word problems by identifying question asked + key words. Demonstrate + underline key words in problem. Create a list of key words with the class. Use txtbk p. 28 WKSHT #19	Aim: Spelling Test Test all 20 short u words	Aim: Locating information using an index. EMPEROR'S SPARROW p 50-55 Voc. dev. oral reading comprehension ck Review seatwork	Aim: Paraphrasing sentences THE FRIDAY FROG 48-53 Seatwork p 17-20 Main Idea p. 10-12 Voc. building p. 12-15

ENDNOTES

1. Meyers, Ellen (Editor): *New Teachers Handbook.* New York: Impact II, 1988, pp. 18–19.
2. Ibid., pp. 19.
3. Anderson, Patricia and Laminack, Lester: "Motivation—The Missing Ingredient." *Early Years,* 1985, *18:* 37.
4. Cornett, Claudia E.: *What You Should Know About Teaching and Learning Styles.* Bloomington: Phi Delta Kappa, 1983, p. 29.
5. Meyers, op. cit., pp. 16–17.
6. Fitzpatrick, Jean Grasso: "Take this Homework Test," *Working Mother,* 1991, p. 52.
7. Canter, Lee: "Homework without Tears," *Instructor,* 1988, *XCVIII:* 29–30.

Chapter Five

GROUPING OPTIONS

To Group or Not to Group? That is the Question.

It is a known fact that students respond to a variety of teaching strategies. Grouping children for instruction is one of these strategies. There are various types of grouping: large, small, teams, pairs, and tutors, each serving a different instructional purpose.

Grouping children for instruction is not an educational panacea. It is merely one way to handle diverse academic achievement in one class. The makeup of each class is unique. You will find great variation in academic achievement, skills and learning styles among your students, as well as within individual students.

In many classrooms children are grouped for reading instruction. In a typical heterogeneous third grade class, there will be a few children at primer and first grade level, a larger group on or about grade level and another group ready for instruction at a fourth or fifth grade level.

In addition, children differ in skill development. One group of children may need help with comprehension skills, another group may require help with word recognition skills, and still another group may need help with study skills.

It would be a waste of teaching time to offer the same instruction to all of these children. Grouping children for instruction is not the perfect way of dealing with academic differences, but it permits the teacher to provide for these differences. Grouping children into smaller groups is closer to individualized reading since the needs of the group is narrowed.

By collecting, compiling and analyzing data on individual students and the class as a whole, you can best determine how students should be grouped to meet their specific learning needs. Standardized test scores will provide you with information on your students' academic strengths and weaknesses. You will also want to give your own informal reading inventory to further assess their abilities. Most standardized tests are given in April and in September you need to evaluate their reading

39

skills before assigning them to a reading group. Your goal is to teach to their strengths and to remediate their weaknesses.[1]

For the new teacher it is best to begin with only two groups and to increase to a maximum of four different groups. After the first two or three years of teaching you will have enough confidence to teach and plan for multiple groups.

How should children be grouped for reading on the basis of reading level?

Instructional Level	Number of Children
Primer	2
First	2
Second	4
Third	12
Fourth	3
Fifth	2

Assume that your third grade class has twenty-five children. The range of reading levels are as above. At first glance, two groups would not really provide for those levels, but two groups are better than one, and three groups are even better!

Two Group Plan	Number of Children
Primer–Second	8
Third–Fifth	17

Three Group Plan	Number of Children
Primer–First	4
Second–Third	16
Fourth–Fifth	5

This is not a firm grouping. As the year progresses, changes will be made. You may even find that after a few weeks you'll need to adjust your groups.

When there's an overlap in achievement levels, it is up to the teacher to find materials which are suitable for the children. Flexibility in the use of materials will reduce the distance between the children's capabilities and your expectations. (Check with a mentor teacher for help selecting appropriate materials.)

Two Group Plan

	Group #1	Group #2
Monday	Independent Activity	Teaching
Tuesday	Teaching	Independent Activity
Wednesday	Teach entire class	
Thursday	Independent Activity	Teaching
Friday	Teaching	Independent Activity

Three Group Plan

	Group #1	Group #2	Group #3
Monday	Independent/Teaching	Teaching/Independent	Independent Activity
Tuesday	Independent Activity	Teaching/Teaching	Independent Activity
Wednesday		Teach Entire Class	
Thursday	Teaching/Independent	Independent Activity	Independent/Teaching
Friday	Independent/Teaching	Teaching/Independent	Independent Activity

Teaching refers to the time you spend teaching a reading lesson to your students. Introducing a new story, vocabulary development, comprehension skills, oral reading, and checking their independent work are some of the activities you will be involved in. Independent activities would include: silent reading, practice exercises, workbook exercises or other activities that relate to previously taught skills or stories.

Group instruction is alternated once a week with whole class instruction. Some types of activities might include: cloze stories, creative dramatics, poetry, reading labs, and newspaper articles. I also read aloud to the class. We enjoyed such classics as: *Tom Sawyer, Arabian Knights* and *King Arthur.* If the children are benefitting from an activity in which all of them can participate, then it is a worthwhile activity.[2]

After you know the children better, you may want to group them according to skills. Vary your groups in number and ability. Also, let them chose their own groups once in a while with a sign up sheet.

How often and in what subject areas you use groups depends on how comfortable you are with grouping students for instruction. Students love working in groups because it is more intimate and they become more involved in the learning process.

Teams are a lot of fun. Students work together and pull together as a team to brainstorm and solve problems. Pairing students together to complete assignments, workbook pages, spelling practice, creative writing, and science projects is another grouping alternative. You'd be surprised how much your students will learn from one another. (Just be sure you know your pairs—don't pair two students who can't get along, or two hotheads together—the results will spell DISASTER.)

Peer tutoring is another method that promotes student achievement. You can use peer tutoring on an informal basis. Whenever you sense that some of the students understand what you've taught and others do not, simply designate "helpers" to go around and help the children who are having trouble.

Peer tutoring can serve to reinforce the skills of the tutor as well as the learner. Peer tutors develop self-confidence and serve as role models for other children.[3]

There are many ways to teach; grouping is one way to vary the approach and reach more children in a more efficient manner.

As I've stated before, the makeup of each class is unique. Within your own classroom you will probably have several: gifted children, learning disabled, one or two special education students who are mainstreamed, one or two "invisible children," in addition to a conglomeration of "average students." You as the classroom teacher must address their needs, as well as the rest of the children. How can you do this in a class of twenty-five? It's not easy, but here are some tips:

Learning disabled students benefit from:

1. Less stimulus—having less problems on a page or covering the ones they are not working on.
2. Repeating directions slowly to assure they hear and understand them.
3. Working on short easy tasks which allows them to meet with success.
4. Lots of positive reinforcement.
5. Use multisensory approaches to subject matter.
6. Constant repetition of learned material.[4]

If you have several gifted students in your class, Virginia Ehrlich has some very practical tips:

1. Ask the gifted the more difficult questions.
2. Let them carry out special research projects related to classwork.
3. Let them work on projects or hobbies that interest them and let them share their work with the class.
4. Let them advance in subjects such as science and math.
5. Let them move on in the basic skills at their own pace regardless of grade level barriers.
6. Let them be free to follow through on advanced work. Many like the challenge of going ahead without assistance.
7. Help them to value their abilities and to feel that they are worthwhile people.
8. Let them make mistakes.
9. Let them know you care.

Please do not:

1. Give them longer assignments for the same topic.
2. Crush their enthusiasm by never calling on them.
3. Ask them to do repetitious and rote tasks.
4. Repress their creativity by rejecting unusual ideas without listening to their explanation.
5. Waste their time on menial tasks.
6. Ask them to tutor others for long periods of time.

Be aware of negative traits in gifted and in learning disabled such as:

1. Excessive restlessness.
2. Mischief making.
3. Poor achievement.
4. Withdrawal, indifference, inattention, and daydreaming in class.
5. Unwillingness to do homework.
6. Persistence in pursuing a discussion or topic beyond the teacher's expressed cutoff point.

Many of these negative traits are sometimes reflections on the nature of the curriculum. Your students may be saying:

1. The curriculum is too easy or too hard.
2. The pace of the classwork is too slow or fast.
3. There are insufficient opportunities for in-depth discussions.

4. The classwork or homework is not challenging or too difficult to sustain interest or attention.
5. The subject matter is uninteresting, too trivial, beneath or above the child's maturity or intellectual scope.[5]

There's one more group of children to note—the "invisible children." They never raise their hands, never ask for help, or never volunteer for projects. They eat lunch alone, play alone at recess and seem to have no friends. There are at least two or three in every classroom. They seem shy, but their loneliness often masks problems: learning disabilities, trouble at home or emotional problems.[6] Their academic work is often close to failing. These children need your special touch; compliments, praise, or a special kindness works wonders. Let them know you are there, you understand, and, when they are ready to talk, you'll listen. I also try to schedule an appointment for myself to meet with the school guidance counselor. First, I discuss what I've observed, then usually the counselor visits the classroom for a short while and then talks with the child privately. Invisible children often become invisible adults. A perceptive teacher can make the difference and you can make that difference.

It is important to remember that every child is an individual. No two children are alike. Each child is unique. It's difficult to meet the needs of every child, but by varying your methods and techniques the task becomes easier.

ENDNOTES

1. Meyers, Ellen, (Ed.): *New Teachers Handbook.* New York, Impact II, 1988, pp. 26–28.
2. Karlin, Robert: *Teaching Elementary Reading: Principles and Strategies.* New York, Harcourt, 1971, pp. 319–322.
3. Steinberg, Adria, (Ed.): "Organizing Classes by Ability." Cambridge, Harvard, 1987, *III:* 1–4.
4. Kirk, Samuel and Gallagher, James: *Educating Exceptional Children.* Boston, Houghton, 1972, pp. 341–343.
5. Ehrlich, Virginia: *Gifted Children: A Guide for Parents and Teachers.* New York, Trillium, 1989, pp. 117–118.
6. Steinberg, Adria (Ed.): "Unpopular Children." Cambridge, Harvard, 1989, *V:* 1–3.

Chapter Six

SUPERVISORY AND
SCHOOL RELATED PERSONNEL

Situation:

Today is your first observation. You are nervous. The supervisor enters your classroom and seats herself in the back of the room. For the next fifteen minutes she makes quiet notes and before your lesson "gets off the ground," she quietly gets up and leaves your classroom. You are upset and disappointed that she won't be able to see your great finish.

It's no wonder the supervisor is often perceived as the enemy. They are seen as an intruder in what a teacher feels is her private domain and each teacher feels she is being graded by this supervisor.

The truth of the matter is that the supervisor is not the enemy, but rather your ally. The job of a supervisor is to help you become a more effective teacher. The students are the center of the classroom. The teacher and supervisor work together with the students' best interest in mind.

No doubt you were observed as a student teacher and you received a grade for your efforts. Now, an unfavorable observation could put your job in jeopardy. One thing you can count on is you will be observed at least once a school year.

Observations

Observations can take many forms. Some are very formal, as clinical observations. This observation technique includes a preconference between the teacher and supervisor. At this conference you will discuss the upcoming lesson, the lesson plan and even specifically what the supervisor will be looking for. This conference allows you to ask questions and narrow down what this observation is to accomplish. For example, if you are having difficulty teaching a particular subject, you may want the supervisor to observe this subject and provide some feedback. Or you may ask your supervisor to provide some feedback on a particular student's behavior. For example, if Joey's lack of interest has troubled you and you've tried to motivate him, but you've been unsuccessful. The supervisor is a trained observer and can sometimes notice things that you have been unable to detect because you are involved in presenting the lesson. After the lesson and observation there will be a post-conference to discuss your lesson and to answer the questions you posed at the preconference.

Not all observations will be quite so formal. Sometimes supervisors will announce that they will be visiting your classroom sometime this week. Other times you will have little or no notice that an observation is in your future. Most of the time you will hear through the "grapevine" that the supervisor has been visiting classes. You may even glance up once from your plan book to find the supervisor has entered your room inconspicuously. If the latter occurs, try not to react to the visitor until later in the lesson. Your supervisor may want to remain anonymous for a while.

Also try not to worry about the students and their behavior. Your students, even those who are uncooperative, will rally to support you and make you look good. They are never quite sure why the supervisor is there to observe you or them, thus the exceptional behavior.

Some teachers like to involve the supervisor in their lesson. A word of caution, some supervisors do not enjoy being put on the spot. I always wait for them to jump in when they are comfortable.

Supervisors are looking for several things when observing your lesson:

1. The aim or objective of the lesson.
2. Were the students motivated?
3. Did you give enough time to the lesson?
4. How did you handle the students? (Call on same students or draw in quieter ones?)
5. Written work, plans or graded papers may be examined to get an overall idea how your students are doing.
6. Some supervisors like to check your room. (My supervisor always checked bulletin boards to see if they were up to date.) Others check the appearance of desks and floors.

There will be a conference and/or an observation form to be signed after the lesson. Most supervisors will review what they observed and make several suggestions on what can be done to improve or expand your lesson.[1] I was once told by a supervisor that my handwriting on the blackboard did not slant enough and that I should practice the correct slant! It may not be easy, but keep your mind open to these suggestions, you can learn from them and nothing pleases a supervisor more than seeing her ideas implemented. On the other hand, if you try these ideas and they do not work discard them. Supervisors understand that not all suggestions will work all the time. By the way, by my next observation my supervisor informed me that my handwriting had a beautiful slant to it! Practice makes perfect.

Supervisors send memos and letters which may or may not require your comments. Supervisors also have meetings that you are expected to attend. This is your chance to be a real professional. Arrive promptly, exercise your good manners and understanding. Some meetings will be more interesting than others, even the dullest conference can provide you with some new teaching insights.

As a new teacher you may find that the supervisor is always in your room. She might stop by once or twice a day for the first month or so. I think this is a good practice for a supervisor. She'll know immediately that you can take control and do your job. If not she'll sense you are in trouble and can help you before it is too late. Always keep in mind that all supervisors were once in your shoes. They all started out as new teachers; they don't forget what that was like—neither will you.

Other School Personnel

When we think about a school we tend to think about students, teachers, and supervisors. But in reality there are many school employees who are a part of the school team. These members include: custodians, food service, para-professionals and school aides, bus drivers, secretaries, nurses, guidance counselors, grounds and maintenance workers, reading specialists, librarians, resource room teachers, speech teachers, security, talented and gifted teachers, social workers, computer operators, and clerical workers. One role depends on another and no one's job is expendable. Thanks to all the members of the school team our schools can run effectively and efficiently, students are happy, there are fewer interruptions, materials are available, and teacher's jobs are automatically much easier because of the atmosphere for effective student learning. The particular personnel make up for each school will vary; you will generally have contact with the following people: para-professionals and educational aides, secretaries, resource room teachers, talented and gifted teachers, the speech therapist, the school nurse, guidance counselors, librarians, custodians, and cafeteria workers. Let's look at each briefly:

Para-Professionals

Educational para-professionals generally work with one or several classroom teachers to assist with these tasks:

1. Instruction and supervision of individual students or small groups.
2. Monitoring and scoring tests and class assignments.
3. Preparation of classroom experiments, projects, demonstrations and visual displays.
4. Operation of audio/visual equipment and computers.
5. Clerical duties such as keeping attendance records.
6. Fee collection and general housekeeping duties.

A para professional can make your job easier. Use them wisely, do not abuse them. Treat them as a colleague, respect them as a professional and you will reap many benefits.[2]

School Secretaries

School secretaries are worth their weight in gold. Your school secretary may keep track of personnel data (absence, lateness, time in, time out, credentials); student data (registration, attendance statistics, transfers); clerical duties (memos, letters, forms, reports, logs and dictations); reception duties (visitors, parents, phone calls, mail and other deliveries); she may even be in charge of the finances (bank accounts, writing checks, and petty cash for emergencies). School secretaries are highly skilled individuals, many have college credits or Associate Degrees from two-year colleges. The school secretary may seem to inundate you with paperwork; keep in mind her job is just as demanding as yours. Grin and bear it! Make her your friend because she knows everything. She holds the keys to your every wish![3]

Out of Classroom Personnel

During those first hectic weeks of school, you will meet several teachers who will be working with some of your students. Each of these teachers will need your help and cooperation not only now, but throughout the school year. These specialists will give you a schedule of days and times they will meet with your students. These programs are called "pull out" programs because the specialist will pull students out of your classroom to work with them.

The Talented and Gifted (TAG) Teacher will take those students who are determined to be gifted. (Each state has a criteria for giftedness — usually high I.Q. of 130 or above, and recommendations from the teacher are also used.) Some schools are fortunate to house a "gifted class" on each grade level, thus eliminating this position. The TAG Teacher will provide a challenging and enriching curriculum for your gifted students. The teacher provides numerous field trips, visual and performing arts experiences in addition to developing critical thinking skills, creativity and research skills.

The Resource Room Teacher works with children who have learning disabilities. Children who score a year or more below grade level on standardized reading and math tests are eligible for these classes. It is the responsibility of this teacher to work with only three or four children on a grade level at a time. This teacher must provide an individualized program for each child which builds on their particular strengths and teaches to their weaknesses.

The Speech Teacher works with students who have speech problems (lisps, and stuttering are two common problems). This teacher has been trained to work with these children to help them communicate better. This teacher can also provide valuable insights and tips for the regular teacher on how to draw these reluctant students into your lessons.

In my school I had two more specialists, the Vocal Teacher for the chorus and the Music Instructor for the band. At times I had less than half my class with all of my students being pulled out for various support services, as they are commonly called. I tried to use these periods for individualized reading and math skills and enrichment activities. In the beginning it is quite disheartening to see your students leave one by one, you worry how will I ever be able to cover the curriculum; you will. You can also take pride in knowing that because of you and these specialists, your students are receiving the best education possible.

School Nurses

School nurses are no longer found in every school. In some districts there is only one nurse who visits all the schools in that district once a month. Some states have regulations forbidding nurses (and teachers) to dispense any medication—even aspirin. Cuts and bruises are usually handled in the school office and, for serious problems, parents are called and the child is taken to the doctor or hospital by the parent. The school nurse must keep accurate records, they will rely on you for some of this information. Height, weight, vision and hearing exams must be recorded on the Health Card as well as dental notes, numerous unexplained absences, and doctors' notes regarding health conditions (hearing problems, asthma and epilepsy). It is important that you keep these records up to date. Your school nurse will be grateful.[4]

Guidance Counselors, Psychologists and Social Workers

These specialists also need information from time to time. Try to supply factual information from your anecdotal records or notes. You may be asked to fill out several reports for different agencies. Keep in mind that this paper work is in the best interest of your students. If you wish to refer a child for counseling, be sure to have your facts ready. File the appropriate forms and you should speak directly to the counselor before the student speaks to the counselor. Acquaint yourself with the guidance personnel early in the school year; they can provide valuable insights into some classroom problems. They also provide literature and up to date research on some common problems.[5]

School Librarians

School librarians expose children to literature, books and the inner workings of the library. Before your first visit, you may want to review "good library manners" with your class. School librarians teach your students how to use the library and its many resources. Most librarians are open to working with you and your curriculum. Therefore, if you assign a science or history report, the librarian will teach your students how and where to begin their research. (Just be sure to give the librarian a week or two of notice.) She can also help you select books and filmstrips to use in your classroom, just for the asking.

Cafeteria Workers

Most schools serve both breakfast and lunch. Cafeteria personnel may not have direct contact with you but they do have direct contact with your students. Cafeteria personnel includes: dietician, cooks, and servers. Although most children gripe at the menus, the menus are well balanced. Sometimes special diets are required for some students and they provide these too. You can also get a good hot meal for a nominal cost. Just send your request to the cafeteria early to assure your lunch will be waiting for you at noon.[6]

Custodial Help

Custodial workers have a tough job. They are on duty all the time. If you have a broken window, jammed lock, forgotten your keys, burnt out a bulb or a student has just vomited, the custodian is there to help. You will learn quickly to have a good relationship with these workers. Be friendly, thankful and cooperative. Empty the baskets when they are full, keep your room neat, straighten desks and put the chairs on top of the desks before leaving for the day. These things will make their job easier and assure you of a clean room.

The Substitute Teacher

Occasionally, you will be out sick or need to take a personal day. Your school will hire a substitute teacher to replace you for the day. (You should know the school policy on sick days well before you need them. Do you call the school? Do you call the substitute directly? How much notice does the school need?) Substitute teachers always come prepared with things for your students to do. They prefer to work from your plans and keep things moving smoothly while you are out. (There's enough disruption not having you there!) Please keep your Plan Book up to date. This will allow them to continue the lessons. It is also a good idea to have a folder in your top drawer marked Substitute Teacher. In this folder keep some review worksheets your students can do while the substitute is getting organized. You may want to add a puzzle or fun worksheet to this folder for the end of the day. Include in this folder any information a substitute may need. Children with health problems, children who are to be dismissed early, a copy of your schedule, fire drill procedures, dismissal information, list of children who take the bus, get hot lunch, go to special programs (TAG, Speech, Resource Room) and any other information you think will help. All of these little things you do now will help her to do a better job and spend more time teaching your class.

A school is not just a physical plant. You will come in contact with many school employees during the course of the school day. The better the relationships between school personnel, the better the atmosphere will be for effective student learning.

ENDNOTES

1. Stoops, Emery, Rafferty, Max and Johnson, Russell: *Handbook of Educational Administration: A Guide for the Practitioner.* Boston, Allyn, pp. 605–607. 1975.
2. A.F.T.: "Your Career as an Education Para-Professional." Washington, D.C., A.F.T., pp. 1–2 1987.
3. P.S.R.P.: "Para-Professionals and School Related Personnel, Education Office Employee, You Have a Tough Job." Washington, D.C., P.S.R.P., p. 4. 1989.
4. Stoops, op. cit., pp. 450–453.
5. Ibid., pp. 564–566.
6. Ibid., pp. 460–466.

Chapter Seven

SURVIVING YOUR FIRST PARENT-TEACHER CONFERENCE

Since parents and teachers are the most important influences in a child's life, it is essential that they coordinate their efforts for the child's best interest. Thus, the parent-teacher conference. This conference can be an excellent opportunity for the teacher to gather information and formulate plans to help your students. You'll be surprised how many day-to-day problems can be solved by these conferences.

The parent-teacher conference has several clear-cut goals:

1. To evaluate the child's progress and plan for continued progress.
2. To help parents understand that you are genuinely interested in helping their child.
3. To get a total picture of the child through giving and receiving information.
4. To learn about the child's home life and factors that may influence the child's behavior.
5. To learn how to view children more objectively.[1]

Parent-teacher conferences are usually held twice a year, once during the fall and then again during the spring semester. The meeting lasts between fifteen and twenty minutes depending upon the number of students in your class and the block of time set aside for the conferences. In order for these conferences to be successful you will need to devote some time preparing for the conference. With a little preparation, you can make parts of your job easier and devote more of your time teaching your students. By being prepared, you will demonstrate to the parents that you are a dedicated professional.

Before the Interview

You can prepare for the conference by reviewing each child's cumulative record card, test record (standardized test scores), class tests, samples of the child's classwork, and any other pertinent data. You may want to put the class tests and samples in a folder and label it with the child's name.

Get yourself a stack of 5" by 8" index cards. On each card write the child's name and record any information you would like to discuss with the parent. For example, record the latest reading and math standardized scores and indicate in red those that are below level. You will want to convey this information to the parents. You will want to record how the child is performing in all academic areas, specify strengths and weaknesses. If a child has a gift or talent in a particular subject area, you might want to include that in your conference notes. Try to include several adjectives to describe each child. For example, "Stephanie is an alert and energetic fourth grader." or "Thomas is an active and enthusiastic learner." This demonstrates to the parent that you do indeed know their child personally and that their child is not just another face in the crowd. By using these index cards you have all the pertinent information at your fingertips—rather than flipping through books and pages, you also appear more professional and polished.

Next you should provide an informal, relaxed setting where you can talk to the parent privately. This is important whether the information you are relaying is good or bad. Each parent is entitled to privacy. If other parents are waiting, cordially invite them to be seated in the hallway outside your room. You may want to have several chairs set up outside your classroom for this purpose. A sign up sheet for parents is also a nice idea unless you are seeing parents by appointment. A sign up sheet not only will keep things moving along smoothly, but it will also provide you with a record of those parents who attended the conference.

On your classroom door you can post a "Welcome Parents" sign. This will help them to feel more comfortable. You could also have your name conspicuously displayed inside and outside the classroom. This will help parents locate the classroom. It will also help them to remember your name. Some parents have several children in the school and will be visiting several teachers and it is easy to get the teacher's names mixed up! You should be ready now to face your first parent conference with confidence.

During the Interview

It is important to keep in mind that the parents you are about to meet are nervous too. They are worried about what you are going to tell them and if you will ask them a question that they won't be able to answer. This may sound funny, but many parents feel threatened by a teacher and perceive you as the teacher they hated when they were in school. Therefore, it is particularly important to show the parents you are not the enemy; you are a friend.

You can begin by greeting the parent in a warm, friendly manner. A smile and a handshake will break the ice.

If you know you will have to be firm with a certain parent, sit at your desk; it suggests authority. Usually, however, you will want to sit in a chair away from the desk; this suggests partnership.

Begin your conference on a positive note by mentioning a strength of the pupil, and use this to convey sincerity and interest. Everyone likes to hear something nice, especially parents.

Avoid rambling and useless discussions by selecting no more than two or three topics to discuss. Keep these purposes in mind throughout the conference. Use your index card to keep you on track.

If you have many parents to see, be sure they understand that the amount of time available for each parent is limited. If time is running short, plan another meeting time with the parent to continue your discussion.

It is important to keep in mind that parents come to these conferences because they are curious about the school and you. Parents want to know in real terms how their child is doing, and how they can help. Try not to use terms that they will not be able to understand. We as educators have a lingo all our own that parents are not privy to. For example, we may refer to a child's gross motor coordination or the child's ability to decode the written word. You'll end up with many blank stares if you use this lingo. Keep the language plain and simple, use phrases such as "getting along with others" rather than the child's "relationship with his peers." In this way parents will understand what you are telling them and you won't be wasting time explaining terminology to them.

Put yourself in the parents' place and try to imagine how you would feel at all points of the conference. Introduce problems tactfully, especially if the parent seems unaware of the problem or is defensive. The goal is to solve the problem, not to "tell on the child." If there's a chance that the child may be held over in the grade, try to get the parents on your side by explaining that now is the time to really learn the basic material so that the child will not be lost later on. Try to make a plan with the parent, not for them. Try to build on constructive elements in the situation rather than picking up on negative aspects of the parent's thinking.

End the conference on a constructive note by summarizing plans for continuing cooperation. Give the parent some time for asking any questions that they may have brought to the conference. If necessary, make another appointment with the parent to meet in a month to discuss any progress. Most parents will be cooperative and really work with you for the benefit of their child. Another conference to discuss progress lets them know the plan is working.

After the Interview

After the interview you should evaluate the conference. Below you will find a checklist to help you. On the same index card record the conference briefly and objectively.

1. How did the parent react?
2. What did I learn that will help me in my relationship with the child in the classroom?
3. Did the parent learn a little more about their child?
4. Did I give the child honest praise as well as tell his shortcomings?
5. Did we arrive at specific ways to help the child?
6. Did I establish a working relationship with the parents?[2]

There's one more party to consider in this matter—the child. Children are often curious and anxious about parent-teacher conferences. Teachers can ease this tension by explaining to their class about what a parent-teacher conference is and what is does for them. It should not be used as a threat by either the teacher or the parent. Discuss the conference with the child. Be positive and tell him about any changes or new plans. Praise him for a job well done, build his self confidence—the better he feels about himself the better he will do in school. After all isn't that what we want for all our students?

Open School Week

Open school week is another way of saying "open house." An invitation is extended by the Principal, to the parents to visit the school and observe their children in the classroom. This is usually done in mid-school year. In some instances there are special presentations, art exhibits, science displays and physical education demonstrations for the parents to attend as well. It really isn't as bad as it sounds; the children love it; they get a chance to "show off."

It will be anything but a typical week for you. Parents will be coming in and out of your room. At times, there will be only one or two parents in your room. Other times, there will be standing room only and you'll wonder where they all came from. Try to make them feel welcome. Put a welcome sign on the door with your name and class. Provide a few adult size chairs in the back of the room, if space allows. You can ask the custodian for the chairs. This way some of the parents will have a seat while others stand. It will make your room seem less crowded this way.

Stay calm. Keep your lesson brief. Provide lots of opportunities for your students to shine. Ask them more questions, have them read aloud or work a math problem at the blackboard. The parents are there to see their child shine. That is unless your parents come to see you teach— mine did! It was an open school that I'll never forget!

Open school week only happens once a year and you will survive. You may even look forward to it next year!

Report Cards

In addition to the parent-teacher conferences, it is the teacher's responsibility to report student achievement to the parents. Report cards are sent home to the parents several times during the school year. Each school system has a report card and a set of standards to which each child is measured. There are basically two styles of reporting student achievement: with symbols, letter or number grades, or with words, written comments on student achievement. It is a good idea to ask your supervisor for reporting guidelines early in the semester. It is important for you to know what standards are being used and why.

Individual teacher comments can be a mixed blessing. You can really express the student's strengths and weaknesses, rather then categorizing a child's ability with a number or letter. On the other hand, if your comments are not clear and simply stated the parents will have little or no idea what the teacher means. For example, if your child's report card said "Susan is not working to her full potential," you as a teacher would understand, but would a parent? Instead the teacher should have said "Susan needs to work harder." You must also be very careful how you word your comments; you certainly do not want to insult or upset the parent.

If you have trouble with comments, there are a number of books available for teachers for just this purpose. They give you various situations and several sample comments to use or build on. Remember when you are responsible for written reports to parents, they must understand what you say, otherwise, they are useless. One year I remember having to write each parent a letter. The school paid for the stationery, but each teacher had to write a letter of evaluation for each child. That year I had thirty-eight third graders. I can't tell you how many hours it took to write and rewrite those letters. It was wonderful for the parents, they loved the letters, but the teachers did not like the fact that they were so time consuming!

Some schools try to make your job a little easier by using number codes that correspond with most used phrases. The only problems with this system is finding a comment that is really what you wanted to say about that child or inadvertently marking one choice because of wording. For example, you may mark five (excellent) when you really meant three (satisfactory) because excellent sounds better and is the truth.

If your school system uses number grades, you must find out the restrictions or limits on grades. (In number grades 65 is passing and in letter grades a D is passing.) Are there special grades used for failing because of absences? (In my school a student received a 44 for excessive absences.) Can you give any number grade? Or must the grades be in denominations of 5? You will not know these little details unless you ask.

Letter grades can be fun too! An A–F system has five categories, (A, B, C, D, and F), yet an O–U system can have three to five categories (outstanding, satisfactory and unsatisfactory; or outstanding, good, satisfactory, unsatisfactory and failing.) It is important when giving letter grades to know how many divisions there are in order to judge a student's achievement accurately.[3] You must also find out if pluses and minuses are acceptable. I served on a report card committee once. We had to design our own report cards and come up with a grading system and divisions. We never discussed pluses and minuses, yet some teachers used them and others did not. You can imagine our embarrassment trying to explain our oversight to the parents. Make sure you know everything about the grading system before you begin.

On some report cards teachers are required to give standardized test results for reading and math. These can usually be found in the Permanent Record Card folder. Be careful to copy these scores exactly onto the appropriate spot on the child's report card.

Permanent Record Cards

Permanent record cards are student profiles. These records are centralized in some systems in the main office or you may find them in your own classroom. Teachers are not required to read student records, but they should read them for the information they contain. There are several areas where you can find this information:

1. Student Health Records—Check these records carefully and early in the school year. You'll recall the story of the child with the hearing problem that was recorded on the wrong card. Check for hearing problems, visual problems, special health problems—asthma is quite common—excessive illness or excessive absences and physical restrictions. Health information plays an important role in learning. By being aware of the child's limitations, you can help make their learning experience more successful.

2. Take a look at absences and lateness. Are they excessive? Are they frequent? Is there a pattern? Serious illness or family problem? If a child is missing a great deal of school it directly affects his classroom performance.

3. Check the child's birthdate. There may be a two-year range in age in your classroom. Has the child been skipped or held over? Did the child enter school early or late? Age can play an important role in a child's social behavior.

4. Check the information section about the child's family. Is it complete? Are addresses and telephone numbers up to date? Are there any brothers or sisters? Is it a single parent family? Have they moved often? These factors have a direct bearing on a child's classroom behavior.

5. Look at all the material in the student's folder. Check student progress in each subject area. Read teacher comments. There may be a "group" I.Q. test, which may provide some further insight into your student's academic background. Individual I.Q. scores are generally

more accurate, but, as with any standardized tests, should be taken lightly. Always keep in mind that on any given day a child may score higher or lower for a variety of reasons.[4]

Permanent records need to be updated at least once a year. Start updating your records early and continue throughout the school year. Check addresses and telephone numbers in September and February. When test results are available, enter them right away; do not put it off. Record height, weight, vision and hearing tests as soon as they are completed. If you do a little work during the year it won't all slide until June. There will be plenty of paper work at the end of the year so play it smart and get a jump on it early in the year. You'll be glad you did!

Anecdotal Records

One last type of record I'd like to discuss is the Anecdotal Record. This is not an official record, such as the Permanent or Health Record. An anecdotal record is an informal record that a teacher keeps during the school year.

I used a small notebook, which I kept in my desk to record various events in my classroom. For example, whenever there was a fight between two students in my class, I would record when, where, and why the fight occurred. Sometimes there is a pattern and you can eliminate the problem. It can be used as documentation for suspension when a child is continuously disruptive. In another instance, I suspected child abuse and kept a record of my observations. My record proved to be quite valuable.

An anecdotal record can prove to be valuable when talking to parents about their child's behavior. You have all the facts written down in your little book. You can tell them exactly when and where the problem occurred. Often a parent can relate a home experience such as death, divorce, illness or a family fight which may have caused a particular outburst. Again, this is not a requirement, but anecdotal records are worth the time you invest in them.

Teacher Report Cards?

When I taught third grade, the class and I created a teacher report card. The children selected the areas in which I was to be graded and then they decided how I was to be graded. I was graded from excellent to unsatisfactory in such areas as: appearance, fairness, homework, friendliness, lesson presentation and questioning techniques. (This was a very bright and perceptive group of children.) It was a wonderful experience for the children to create a report card and grading system. They found it wasn't so easy to grade the teacher. They learned what teachers go through every marking period. I told them to be honest, that I would take their comments seriously, and I did. I learned that I wasn't perfect; there were a few areas in which I needed to improve. I gave too much homework and I always called on the same students, some of my lessons were even boring! From time to time I'd review my report cards to see if I'd improved and by June I passed with flying colors. It was a wonderful learning experience for all of us.

I would recommend trying this exercise after a few years of teaching, when your ego can handle the blow. I recommend trying it with a bright, responsible group of students who will love the challenge!

ENDNOTES

1. National Education Association: *Conference Time for Teachers and Parents.* Washington, D.C., N.E.A., 1984, pp. 4–7.
2. Long, James, Frye, Virginia H., Long, Elizabeth W.: *Making It 'Till Friday: A Guide to Successful Classroom Management.* New Jersey, Princeton, 1989, pp. 97–103.
3. Ohles, John: *Introduction to Teaching.* New York, Random House, 1970, pp. 200–202.
4. Ibid., p. 181.

Chapter Eight

THE INFAMOUS CLASS PLAY

Setting A Class Play

Does the thought of a class production scare you or at least cause several sleepless nights? School productions are notorious for causing anxiety in teachers and students alike. The fact is you will be responsible for a minimum of one class production during the school year.

A class production involves your students: intellectually, emotionally, physically, verbally and socially. As actors in a play, children assume the roles of others, which allows them to learn about others' problems, solutions and values that may be different from their own. Children learn to interact, cooperate and work together toward the final product—the production. As you can see, a class production does have its educational merits.

You, as the teacher, will also gain some new insights from this experience. A class production will reveal many hidden talents, not only theatrical, but social skills as well. Before you begin you will need a time frame. For younger children, I would allow two to four weeks from the onset to the completed production. For older children and a more elaborate production, four to six weeks should be enough time to get it all together.

One word of caution. Try not to fall prey to the Romeo and Juliet syndrome. This syndrome is common amongst new teachers. In order to impress the supervisor (and colleagues) new teachers try a major performance, such as Romeo and Juliet, the Sound of Music or West Side Story. These elaborate productions usually end in disaster. Keep it simple your first year. There are many excellent plays for children that are easy to perform and will impress your supervisor and colleagues.

Scene One, Act One

Choosing the Script

The formal play is primarily audience centered. A script is either written or selected in advance and memorized by the players. Most teachers select a formal play for their class to perform. With children in the lower grades it is best if the children present a play based on something they know or have learned. It can even be written by the students with your guidance. For example, if your class has been studying New York City, they can dramatize material relating to it, the play then emerges from this material. Add some slides, narration, music and dance and you've got yourself a class production. Or the class may decide to dramatize a story they have read and enjoyed. My fourth grade class enjoyed the story, *Snoopy Gets Married,* by Charles Schultz. We wrote the dialog together, added a few scenes, added some female roles and even changed the ending so we could celebrate Snoopy's Wedding in style. The play was a huge success due to their enthusiasm, they were proud of themselves and I was proud of them myself.

Sometimes, a class will want to do a play that is not related to the curriculum. They want to try a "real play" with a traditional script. There are many "play" books available to you at your school, public or university library. Subject matter and age group will vary. Ask the librarian for help in selecting the books that will be of value to you. One problem you may encounter will be to find a good script that will offer many acting opportunities for your students. Many scripts feature four or five main characters and are either female or male dominated. You may need to adapt the play by adding a scene or more characters to the existing cast. Everyone wants a part—at least a line to say in the play, so keep this in mind when you make your selection.

Scene One, Act Two

Casting the Play

Once you select or write the play, your next task will be to cast the play. The matter of casting is important. The teacher should try to get the best possible cast together. This can be done in two ways.

You can assign parts to your students. When the children are young this is the easiest. You know the children best and you know who should play the giant and who should play the dwarf or elf based on their physical characteristics. To cast students because they are bright or verbal is not a fair practice. Children pick up on this very quickly, so be very careful.

There may be a child or two who prefers not to be cast in a major role.

You should consider their request, and investigate the reason behind the request before deciding.

Casting can also be done by means of try outs or auditions. This works well with older children, they love to audition. The hard part is deciding who deserves the role. You will have your work cut out for you. Here's how to proceed:

First, give everyone a copy of the script to read through. Give them a night or two to decide which part they would like to audition for and allow them to sign up for that part. Select a day and time for try outs. Then sit back and listen to the auditions carefully, take notes. Let them know how long it will take you to make your decisions. When you make your announcements be positive. Let them know how proud you are of all of them and how difficult the decision was to make because they were all so talented. When a child auditions, he opens himself to teasing and criticism from his peers. For this alone, they deserve our praise. Naturally, there will be some children who are disappointed, but there will also be lots of excitement.

Once the casting is complete, you can set a date by which all their lines must be memorized. One or two weeks is usually sufficient time depending on the age group and length of the production. Meanwhile you can start rehearsing the play using the script. You will find that there are a few children in every class who choose not to be on the stage for the production. I try not to force them. I want this to be a pleasant experience for everyone. Instead I get them involved with the programs, invitations and scenery. In this way they are an important part of the production team without the stress of getting on stage. I do ask them to take a bow at the end of the production with the rest of the class.

Scene One, Act Three

Costumes

One of the very first questions your students will ask will be about costumes. Will I get to wear a costume? Can my mother/grandmother make me a costume? Or what shall I wear for a costume?

The subject of costumes can be a source of worry for both the teacher and her students. There will be students who will have parental help and support. There will also be students who do not have this help. The teacher can try to solve the matter of costumes by suggesting that the students adapt some of their garments to the play. If everyone wears dark pants and white T-shirts, you can then add hats, aprons, shawls, boots, scarves and jewelry to suggest various types of characters. Children welcome simple suggestions and so will their parents. The simpler the costumes the better, the children will be more comfortable and there will be less fidgeting![1]

Scene One, Act Four

Scenery, Lighting, Music and Props

Scenery. Scenery means the background that suggests the locale of the play. If the play takes place inside a house, a table, chairs and some painted scenery would suggest such a setting.

The art department can help with the painted scenery. Your artistic students can also design scenery and do not rule out parents, grandparents, aunts/uncles or siblings. Be sure to tap all possibilities. Here are a few tips:

1. Scenery should not get in the way of the actors.
2. Scenery should be simple and suggest the time and place of the scenery.
3. Scenery should be strong, not flimsy and enhance the production.

Children have wonderful imaginations and can suggest some good ideas for scenery. Work closely with them, they can be a valuable asset.

Scenery is usually not needed until the final week of rehearsals. This will give the actors a chance to work with it before the actual performance.

Lighting. Lighting will depend on what is available in your school. Perhaps there will be a few simple spotlights, or maybe some stage lights. Lighting equipment is dangerous and expensive, therefore it is best if you or another adult take charge of this job. Take the time to learn about the equipment and practice, practice, practice.

Music. Music always enhances a performance. If you're not musical you can still have music as part of your program. You can ask the music teacher to accompany you on the piano. You can have the school band play music for your program. You may even have several students in your class who play musical instruments and they can play for the performance. Another alternative is to use a record, cassette tape or compact disk. I wanted to use the song "New York, New York" at one of my performances, but the music teacher was not available. I made a copy of the song and played the cassette tape at the performance. If you use taped music or a record, be sure to have an extra copy of the tape or record and check the machines they will be played on before the performance. Be sure to include extra time for music rehearsals before adding it to the play rehearsals.

Properties. Properties is the formal name given to props, the small objects used by the players. Dishes, swords, baskets, telescopes and guns are some popular props. Props should be collected before and after each rehearsal and kept in one place. Begin collecting these properties well before the performance in order to allow the actors time to get used to handling them.

Scene Two, Act One

Directing

Once rehearsals begin you begin your new role as director. Directing is not as difficult as it sounds. You need to give the cast enough direction to make them feel comfortable yet be open to individual interpretation. (Remember that acting is an art form.) The script usually gives clear directions, but it will be up to you to make the final decisions. You may need to develop "hand signals" to help your students with entrances, exits, movements (move to the front of the stage), and for speaking loudly. You'll also be responsible for supplying the words when the actors forget their lines.

Scene Two, Act Two

Rehearsals

As the director, you will need to set up the performance date and a rehearsal schedule. Check with your supervisor regarding the date and time of the performance. Also arrange to use the auditorium for your rehearsals and dress rehearsals. Keep in mind that rehearsals should be frequent, but short. At first, rehearse specific scenes, complete run through will come later.

During the rehearsals you will need to plan the movements of the actors. You should know in advance when characters enter and leave, and where they sit or stand to deliver their lines. Discuss these moves with the actors so they can learn why they need to enter and exit as you suggest.

Next, you will need to discuss individual actions that each character performs. The actors need to understand that their sweeping, sewing, eating, fighting and cleaning actions are not merely something to do. These actions help the audience to believe the character they are playing. This is also a good chance to introduce props and to have the characters get used to them.

As the director you will need to watch the entire performance unfold in front of you. Do the actors hide each other? Talk too low? Is the scenery in the way? Is the stage too crowded? Does the music flow? Is there enough room for the dancers? Does the performance flow? It will with practice, practice, practice.

Scene Two, Act Three

Before the Dress Rehearsal

Understudies are recommended for all major roles. It doesn't happen often, but once in a while one of the main characters will get sick. For the class and the teacher, this can be quite upsetting. If you have an understudy in the wings, you'll be prepared to go on with the show!

Parent helpers are another asset. If you can get two or three parents to help behind the curtain or in the wings, your job out front will be easier. Parents can help with the lighting, getting the actors dressed and backstage behavior control. You need reliable help behind the curtain to ensure a smooth production.

You may want to give some thought to invitations and programs. Invitations can be written and designed by your students. They can be given to each classroom teacher, stating the date and time of the performance. They can also be given to the parents, inviting them to a special performance.

A program is not necessary, but some classes enjoy designing them. Parents love them, they love to see their child's name in print. The decision is ultimately yours. If you have the time and energy, you may want to consider this option.

Scene Two, Act Four

The Dress Rehearsal

The dress rehearsal is the culmination of everyone's effort. There should be at least two dress rehearsals. The first one should be with the scenery in place, and the second with costumes. After each rehearsal costumes and props should be put away carefully.

If makeup is used it too should be tried out at the dress rehearsal. Before using any makeup on children, be sure their parents have been consulted. Have plenty of cold cream and makeup remover available.

The Performance

The big day has arrived, you are ready for your first performance. Your attitude will have the greatest impact on your students. Be calm and encouraging. This will ease their anxiety and help your students to look forward to the performance with anticipation.

Before the performance be sure to:

1. Check all costumes and props.
2. Check that the actors are comfortable.
3. Check the scenery, lighting, music and any machines you will be using during the performance.
4. Check to see if the auditorium is set up and comfortable. If you are using a slide or film projector be sure the shades are drawn.
5. Give your class a pep talk and any final thoughts you may want to share.
6. Relax, you've done your best to prepare for this day. Everything will turn out fine. Just wait and see.
7. Be sure to collect photos of the performance. It is great to be able to look back and remember. If your school has a video camera, see if you can arrange to have the performance videotaped. (Perhaps one of the parents may videotape the performance and make a copy for you.) The children love to see the performance on videotape. It is a real thrill.[2]

Last, if your school allows, throw a cast party. Let your class know that they've done a wonderful job—CELEBRATE!

Alternatives

There are several alternatives to the class play:

1. Choral Speaking
2. Poetry and Songs
3. A Circus

Choral Speaking

Choral Speaking is simply reading or reciting in unison under the direction of a leader. It is a group art. Its merits include:

1. It works well with groups of any size or age.
2. Encourages group participation.
3. Can bring shy and handicapped children into the limelight.
4. Promotes good speaking skills in an enjoyable fashion.
5. Provides an opportunity to introduce poetry.[3]

Some good poetry choices would be:

HALLOWEEN	BY GERALDINE BRAINE SIKS
MY SHADOW	BY ROBERT LEWIS STEVENSON
THE WIND	BY ROBERT LEWIS STEVENSON
STOPPING BY WOODS ON A SNOWY EVENING	BY ROBERT FROST

Poetry and Song

Poetry and song work very well together. Poetry grew out of dance and song so they are very compatible. If you pick a theme first, your task will be even easier. Spring, Pets are Wonderful, or Halloween all work quite well. Select several poems and songs to go with your theme. Work on the poetry first. Assign an entire poem or just a verse to groups of students. Once they have mastered the poetry, introduce the songs. Introduce the songs, one at a time. For the performance, intertwine the poetry and songs. Scenery can be simple, as well as costumes. You can use choral speaking as a grand finale. It may sound simple, but the results are outstanding!

A Circus

Another clever alternative to a class play is to stage a circus. Many teachers find this choice appealing. It allows them to introduce the topic of a circus, and explore it, historically, creatively and physically.

This performance will require a great deal of work. Try to enlist the help of the P. E. teacher to help your students develop the physical skills necessary to perform in a circus. Among the skills you can develop are:

Juggling Acts — Have the children learn to juggle from one to four balls. Older children can try juggling rings.

Stilts — You can create stilts by using two tin cans and tying string through them. Be careful to file down any rough edges found on the cans. Ask the children to be careful as they walk about on their stilts.

Clown Act — Everyone wants to be a clown just for the fun of it. Give them some water guns and shaving cream pies and you've got a clown act.

Animal Act — Children can pretend they are wild animals in a circus. They can march around, jump through a hula hoop or beg for food.

Balancing Act — This can be done with a small balance beam which the strong man must set up on stage. What wondrous things your students will do on this beam and without a net!

Acrobatics — Great for students who take gymnastics. They can do forward and backward rolls, head stands and cartwheels.

Magician — Here you can include some very simple magic tricks.[4]

With some music and sound effects and let's not forget the ring master, you've got yourself a mini circus and an unforgettable performance.

Conclusions

There is probably nothing that brings a class closer together than a class production. It creates lasting memories for all who share in it. Your first production will be most memorable, so get out there and make some memories!

ENDNOTES

1. Heining, Ruth: *Creative Drama for the Classroom Teacher* K–3. New Jersey, Prentice-Hall, 1987, pp. 201–205.
2. McCaslin, Nellie: *Creative Drama in the Classroom.* White Plains, Longman, 1990, pp. 362–381.
3. Dallmann, Martha: *Teaching the Language Arts in the Elementary School.* Dubuque, Wm. C. Brown 1976, pp. 310–314.
4. McCaslin, op. cit., pp. 400–412.

Chapter Nine

YOUR FIRST CLASS TRIP

(Or, If This is Wednesday, We're Off the Zoo!)

A re you ready for your first class trip? I bet you're excited; I was! I bet you are a wee bit nervous too. A class trip is a major undertaking, not to mention the responsibility of removing thirty students from the safe confines of the school grounds to set them loose in the big city. Don't let a class trip scare you; after your first class trip you'll be a veteran.

There is no simple formula for a successful class trip. A good result requires time, effort and care. There are no shortcuts when it comes to traveling with children. You must learn how to preplan, organize, and take that trip, so buckle up and let's get started.

Purpose

A class trip can have many purposes, but its aim or objective should be educational. Your lesson plans begin with an aim, so should your class trip. This does not mean that class trips cannot be fun. A class trip will be what you make it.

There are several types of class trips:

1. Trips that are related to your curriculum. A visit to the planetarium to learn more about the night sky.
2. Trips that are designed to motivate learning. You are beginning a unit on sea life. A trip to a local tropical aquarium will spark their curiosity as they discover various types of fish.
3. Trips that will affect your student's behavior. Learning about the community. A special project might involve shopping in a local store for cooking supplies. The cooking may be your planned outcome, but they learn to shop, purchase, use money and interact socially.
4. Trips that culminate a unit. A movie version of a book they've finished or a visit to an on-stage production of a classic they've read.

Planning

Once you have decided on the educational purpose and destination of the class trip, the real planning begins.

First, work out the details of the trip. Decide the where, when and how to get there. Make the trip yourself before you even suggest the idea to your students. Taking the trip first enables you to consider the following:

1. Transportation options—school bus or public transportation including costs and time element.
2. Admission costs and payment procedures. Do they need a deposit? Do they accept cash or a check?
3. Location of the bathrooms. Once you get there someone will need to make a stop. Are they centrally located or out of the way?
4. Cafeteria facilities. You will need to have lunch while you're there. Will you use their facilities? Can the students bring a bag lunch? Is there a place to picnic if the weather is nice?
5. Maps or Guides. Do they supply you with a tour guide or do you need a map for a self-guided tour? If you need maps, now is the time to get them.
6. Location of the Gift Shop. No class trip is complete without a trip to the gift shop for some souvenirs.
7. Time to tour. Take the tour yourself and get an idea of how much time you will need to visit this facility?
8. Cameras. Are they permitted and are there any restrictions to their use?

If you cannot make the trip, see if you can get this information from someone on the trip sight.

Next plan the pace of the trip. You have all the facts and you want to assure that everyone will see and do everything without being rushed. This includes stopping for lunch, bathroom stops and souvenir shopping. Try to plan your trip to the gift shop late in the day. Select one vendor or store for the entire class. This way they can look forward to this aspect of the trip and they won't lose their purchases before they leave.[1]

Preparing the Class

Your class will rejoice at the mere mention of a class trip. Now is the time to have a class discussion about trips.

First, discuss the trip you are about to take. Let them know where they are going, why they are taking the trip, and what they will do or see there.

Next, a class discussion on appropriate behavior outside the classroom. You can outline these details for younger children or brainstorm some rules with older students.

You will need to discuss:

1. What type of dress is appropriate for this trip?
2. What items can and cannot be brought on the trip? (Cameras, lunch, snacks, money)
3. When permission slips and money will be due?
4. How to line up for a head count?
5. How much money can be brought?
6. How to act with a guide or parent chaperone?
7. Proper behavior on the school bus or public transportation.
8. Procedures for using the bathroom.
9. Procedure if lost, sick or hurt on the trip.
10. Lunch procedures if buying lunch or bringing a bag lunch.
11. Seating plan for the bus. Children usually sit with a partner. Whoever gets the window on the way to the facility the other child gets the window on the way back.
12. Identification tags for younger children.

The more your students know the easier they will be able to follow your plans.[2]

After this discussion leave time for questions. Be patient. Your students are excited and may need to have things repeated. I also review all procedures again the day before the trip for reinforcement.

Chaperones

My personal philosophy is the more the merrier. Rule of thumb is usually one adult for eight children. If you have younger children you may want to take one adult for five children. You should invite the parent volunteers (even Dads) to meet with you briefly before the trip.

You may have a list of class parents who have already consented to attend the class trips or you can have the parents who are interested in chaperoning send you a note. At this meeting you can give them the following information:

1. List of students they will be responsible for.
2. Briefly outline their duties.
3. Supply them with necessary maps, guidebooks or details about the trip.
4. Expected student behavior and consequences.[3]

I always follow up with a personal thank-you note to each parent volunteer. Parents are busy people, some even take time off from their jobs to be a part of the class trip. I am always thankful for their time and help. Remember that parents are a help, but, as in your classroom, you are in charge of solving the problems. You are the final authority.

I've had some wonderfully successful trips. I've also had some class trips I'd like to forget.

One of my trips began with me spilling an entire cup of coffee all over one the chaperones.

A trip to the circus resulted in a late return to school, because several students ate too much and became sick on the bus. (A trip I will long remember!)

A trip to the airport resulted in the near arrest of one of my chaperones. One of the Dad's was an off-duty police officer, who was carrying his gun, unbeknownst to me. Part of the tour included the class passing through the metal detector. You can imagine our surprise when he set off the metal detector and he had to show proper identification for carrying a gun. Two years later I had his daughter in my class and I had forgotten about the gun incident. This time we went on a trip to the United Nations and, yes, he set off the metal detector again!

Good or bad, a class trip allows you to see your students (and parents) in a new light. The trip gives them a chance to share a new and exciting experience. It teaches them to become a part of the community. The benefits for your students are numerous.

Some schools require a certain amount of trips be taken during the school year. Others have no restrictions as to the number of trips you make. During your first year, three trips are enough; you may want to add a trip or two during the next school year.

I always plan my trips with the help of my class trip checklist which I've included in this chapter. You can work with this list or develop one of your own.

Enjoy your class trips and enjoy your students. This is an educational experience you and your students will long remember.

Class Trip Checklist

Details

1. Decide educational objective of trip.
2. Decide on your destination.
3. Make trip on your own or gather information from someone that works there. Find out:
   a. If reservations are necessary.
   b. The cost of admission.
   c. Are there special hours for class trips?
   d. Do they have guided tours or self-guided tours?
   e. Location of the cafeteria, rest rooms and gift shop.
   f. Any special dress necessary?
   g. Are cameras allowed?

Transportation

1. Decide which type of transportation you will be using.
2. Find out the cost and who pays. Sometimes a school receives free passes for public transportation.
3. If a school bus is needed, what is the procedure for reserving one? Are there time limits on the bus? Some buses must be back at your school by two o'clock in order to take some children home.
4. How will the bus be paid for: check or cash. Is a deposit necessary? Should the driver be tipped?

Permission

1. Fill out appropriate school forms for class trips. Find out how far in advance you must file.
2. Notify your supervisor in writing.

3. Get parental permission slips to be filled out and distributed to your students. Find out the procedure for children who do not have parental permission to attend the trip.

Preparations

1. Explain the trip and its purpose to your students.
2. Discuss proper behavior outside the classroom.
3. Select and prepare chaperones.
4. Seating plan for the bus.
5. Assignment preparation. Something for your students to do when on the trip. Something to look for or questions to answer.
6. Follow up activities. You may want to include:
   a. creative writing
   b. class collage
   c. diary of events
   d. bulletin board
   e. art activity
   f. log of events
   g. snapshot album
   h. dramatization

Evaluation

1. What went well; what didn't?
2. What would you change or do differently?
3. Student evaluation

Write everything down for future reference.

Sample Permission Slip

PERMISSION SLIP

Date _____

I hereby give my consent for my daughter/son to attend the
(circle one)

class trip to the _____ on _____.

Sincerely yours,

_____
Parent's Signature

LET'S PARTY!

About six weeks into the school year, your students will start to ask if they can have a Halloween Party.

Before you answer this question, check with your supervisor about school policy on holiday and other parties. If you get the green light here are some guidelines for class parties:

Party Planner

1. When will the party take place? (date and time)
2. Where will the party be held? (classroom or school basement?)
3. Will there be decorations?
   a. Will they be bought or made?
   b. Who will decorate? Who will clean up?
4. Will there be costumes?
   a. Will they be worn to school or will your students change in the classroom?

5. Will there be refreshments?
   a. Will they be brought or bought?
   b. If they are brought, who will bring what?
   Paper goods—plates, napkins, cups, paper towels.
   Beverages—juice, soda, punch or milk.
   Food—chips, pretzels, cookies, cupcakes, fruit, cheese.
6. How will it be served? Students help themselves or students will serve food?
7. Who will clean up after the party?
   Check with the custodians about clean up. How would they like the trash handled?
8. Will there be entertainment?
   a. Will your students perform?
   b. Will there be music?
      1. Will it disturb other classes?
      2. What audio/visuals will be necessary?
      3. Who will bring the records, tapes or cds?
      4. Who will be in charge of selecting and playing the music?
      5. Will there be dancing? If so, an area needs to be cleared away for a dance floor.
   c. Will there be games?
      1. Who will bring the games? (Monopoly, Clue)
      2. Will there be class games (Pin the tail, apple bobbing)
      3. Who will be in charge?
      4. Will there be prizes? Where will the prizes come from?
9. Cleanup—Procedures and volunteers to pick up and restore the room into a classroom.[4]

These are only guidelines. I'm sure after your first party you will add to this list.

One important suggestion. Be sure to involve the students in the planning. Even in the early grades, students have more fun when they have participated in the planning. Use your guidelines to help them. Keep a written record of who is doing what. You may want to include a quick word about "putting on their party manners." Enjoy your party. Parties are a great way to get to know your students. You'll be astounded as to how many "party animals" you have in your class.

ENDNOTES

1. Butler, Arlene Kay: *Traveling With Children and Enjoying It.* Chester, Globe Pequot, 1991, pp. 21–23.
2. Portnoy, Stanford and Portnoy, Joan: *How to Take Great Trips with Your Kids.* Boston, Harvard Common, 1983, pp. 80–86.
3. Borders, Earl Jr.: *The Bus Trip Handbook.* New Jersey, Home Run, 1985, pp. 17–22.
4. Freeman, Lois M.: *Betty Crocker's Parties for Children.* New York, Golden Press, 1964, pp. 22–29.

Teacher's Prayer

Lord, Please help me
To strengthen their voices,
    bodies and minds.
To express their feelings
    and control them sometimes,
To explore what's near
    and venture afar.
But most important to love
    who they are.

Patsy Moore

Chapter Ten

THE TRUTH ABOUT . . . BULLETIN BOARDS

Colorful, Bright Bulletin Boards Motivate Student Learning

Believe it or not, bulletin boards are not merely a classroom decoration. They are a very valuable and effective teaching tool. (This is a well kept secret!) If you look around any school you will find that most bulletin boards are used as a showcase to exhibit students' work. With just a little imagination and the right supplies, you can turn an ordinary bulletin board into a creative presentation of subject matter. Want to know how? Read on.

The type of bulletin board you'd like to design is called an interactive bulletin board. Aptly named because the students will interact with the material that has been presented on it. It can be used to introduce new material or review previously taught skills. It can be used in all classrooms at all grade levels. Let's look at a few examples.

An early childhood teacher decided her first graders needed to review number words. She cut out twelve large teddy bears and twelve small teddy bears. She wrote the numbers one through twelve on the small bears and the number words for one to twelve on the large bears. She stapled the large bears up on the bulletin board leaving space for each matching smaller bear. She put the small bears and some bulletin board tacks in an envelope attached to the bottom of the bulletin board. The teacher gave her bulletin board a title and wrote simple instructions as a final step.

Once the board was completed the teacher used the board to re-teach the number words. Several students matched the Mamma Bears and the Baby Bears until the board was complete.

Now the board can be left as is for a few days or take down the Baby Bears and put them back in the envelope. You can explain at this time the procedure for future use.

Another elementary school teacher has developed a geography unit on the United States. Her bulletin board is a map of the United States with each state outlined. Her first objective is to have her students recognize the shape and name of each state. In a large envelope she has cut the shape of each state and written the name of the state in marker. The students match each state and tack it to the board. Later the teacher decided to teach state capitols. These were color coded and added to the envelope. She adds major cities, industries and products at a later date.

I remember a bulletin board where I presented a lesson on the various types of sentences (Statement, Question, Exclamatory and Command). At the bottom of the bulletin board in a folder were several different worksheets. The students could visit the bulletin board and take a worksheet back to their desk, when their other work was completed. Worksheets included the following skills: identifying the four types of sentences, writing each type of sentence, and punctuating each type of sentence.

A bulletin board on the solar system can stimulate research on the planets, through the use of worksheets. Later the children present their findings and provide information to the class. For example, one worksheet asked the student to provide five facts about the planet Venus and gave the student three choices of presentation, an illustrated story, a poem or a dramatization. One student was quite creative and became a singing, dancing Venus!

If you'd like to try an interactive bulletin board, here are a few things to keep in mind:

1. Find a bulletin board that can be adjusted to the height of your students or keep their interactions near the bottom where they can reach.
2. Select an area that is easily accessible. It will become a high traffic area.
3. Develop, discuss and post rules for using the bulletin board. Include: who can use it, when, how many children at one time, time limits, or scheduled use, proper use of materials, returning materials and correction procedures.

You may want to consider creating an answer key for the worksheets and bulletin boards, so they can check their own work. Or if they work in pairs they can correct each other's work before submitting it to you.[1]

Not all of your bulletin boards will be interactive. Some will be informative: announcing activities, upcoming events or record various events. Others will be decorative and a showcase for your students' work.

You can use smaller bulletin boards for announcing events: trips, lunches, assemblies, or recording activities such as Our Trip to the Bronx Zoo or Our Trip to the Museum of Natural History. I used smaller boards for daily/weekly schedules, a class job board and a class birthday board. I also had bulletin boards which were seasonal or had a holiday theme. These are tricky because not all children celebrate the same holidays, so be sensitive to all cultures and religions in your class and be sure that they are all represented.

A great deal of time and effort goes into planning an effective bulletin board and having the right materials will make the job easier. Here are a few essentials: Bulletin board paper, lettering, border paper, scissors, stapler, staples, staple remover, markers, tacks and ideas.

Bulletin board paper comes in various widths and lengths and is available in about twenty different colors. It is used primarily to cover the cork.

Letters are available in various styles and sizes. (2″, 4″, and 5″) Letters also come in a variety of colors and textures. Some need to be stapled, others push right into a cork bulletin board. Lettering is an integral part of the display. Keep it legible and concise.

Bulletin board borders are also known as bordette or trimmers. These are used to decorate around the edge of the bulletin board. They come in many colors, styles and designs. They are not necessary, but add a polished look to your boards.

Every well dressed bulletin board needs just the right accessories. Scissors, stapler, staples, staple remover and some bulletin board tacks are vital to a well dressed bulletin board.

All of these materials can be purchased through educational supply catalogs or from the local teaching store.

If you would like to try a more creative and less expensive approach, here are a few suggestions:

Bulletin Board Paper Alternatives

gift wrap	wall paper remnants
aluminum foil	party table cloths
crepe paper	cellophane
contact paper	fabric
burlap	oaktag
construction paper	

Bulletin Board Bordette Alternatives

roll crepe paper	wide ribbon
paper dolls	oak tag
wall paper border	leave the cork show

You can select any design you like, measure and calculate the number of panels you will need. Make photocopies to duplicate the pattern, trim and color with bright markers. Laminate with clear contact.

Lettering Alternatives

string or yarn	glitter
cotton balls	pipe cleaners
newspaper and	felt
magazine letters	ice cream sticks
fabric	contact paper
toothpicks	

Where do all those great bulletin board ideas come from? Some teachers are very creative and design their own boards, others use a variety of resources. These include: bulletin board books, teaching magazines, curriculum guides, textbooks, and bulletin board clubs. You can also purchase bulletin board sets from the teacher's store. These even come with a teacher's guide to assist you with various designs.

The composition of your bulletin board is an important element to consider (Figures 3a–d). The effectiveness of a bulletin board depends greatly on its arrangement. Each board can have its own personality with different colors, textures and layouts.[2]

If you want a really different looking bulletin board you should try a 3-D bulletin board. You can enliven any bulletin board by making letters, pictures, papers or objects three dimensional by adding springs. Here's how:

Cut strips of construction paper wide enough to support the object. Tape two strips together at a right angle. Fold one strip accordion style, tape the unfolded strip to the object. Then staple to the board. The spring will give the object a bouncy effect.

Small cereal boxes and sturdy paper loops can also be used to make objects stand away from the bulletin board.[3]

Interactive bulletin boards may require a pocket or folder. Take one manila folder and cut the tab side horizontally, leaving about two-

Figure 3a–d. The following four illustrations show different bulletin board compositions. Each one presents a unique arrangement.

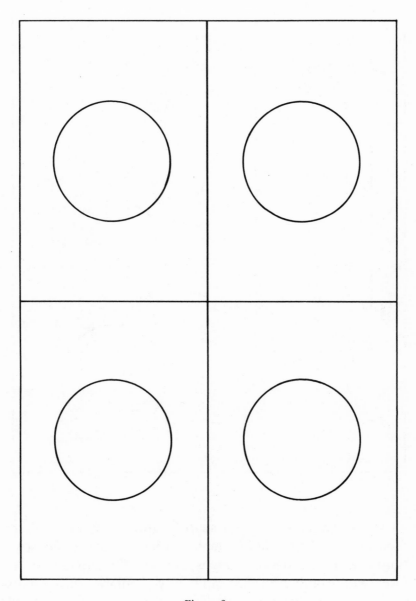

Figure 3a.

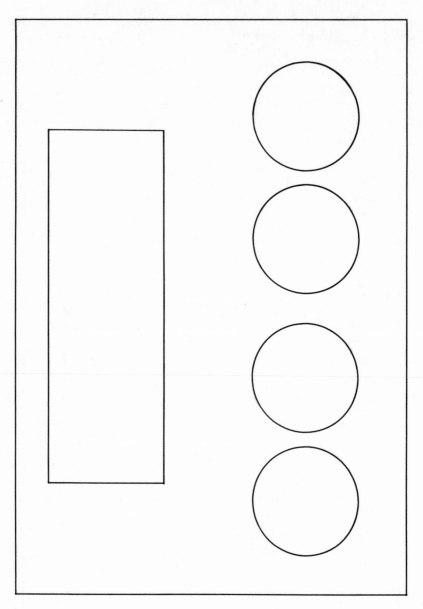

Figure 3b.

thirds. Cut the tab piece into four strips. Staple two to each side of the folder loosely. Cover the front of the folder with contact or construction paper and label it. Business envelopes also work, but are less durable.

An overhead or slide projector can help you enlarge objects to use on a bulletin board. To enlarge a map of the United States use an overhead

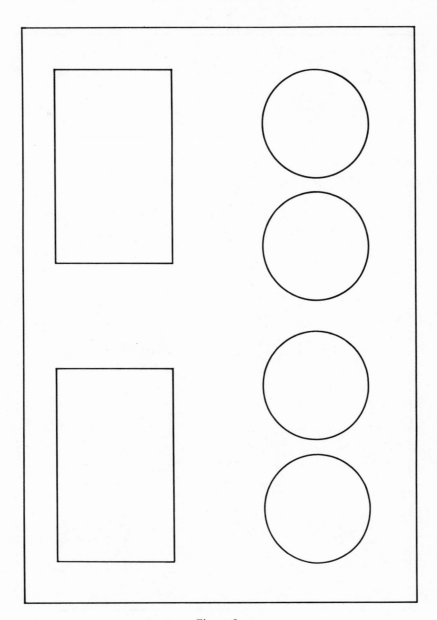

Figure 3c.

projector to project the map onto a large sheet of paper. Trace around the image with a pencil or marker.[4]

Here are some other helpful hints:

1. Purchase fadeless bulletin board paper which can be used over and over again.

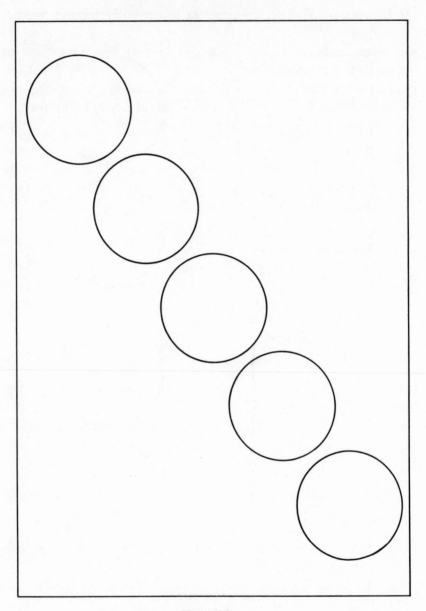

Figure 3d.

2. Change the paper only three times a year. September — November use fall colors. December — February use winter colors. March — June use spring colors.
3. Save all your bulletin board ideas, pieces and letters for the future. You never know when you'll need them.

4. Use staples and staple remover to carefully remove your letters and pieces.
5. Assess bulletin boards carefully—remember interactive boards cause a great deal of traffic.
6. Get students to help you. If your students are too young, perhaps some children in an upper grade would like to help you.
7. Use your resources to gather new ideas:

> Mailbox Education Center, Inc.
> 1607 Battleground Avenue
> P.O. Box 9753
> Greensboro, NC 27499-0123

> Classroom Beautiful
> Bulletin Board Club
> 1607 Battleground Avenue
> P.O. Box 9753
> Greensboro, NC 27499-0123

> SchoolDays
> P.O. Box 2853
> Torrance, CA 90509-2853

Bulletin boards are a great asset to any classroom. Anyone visiting your room, parents, teachers and supervisors and even other students can tell a great deal about you as a teacher by your bulletin boards. Keep them neat, clean and up to date. Be creative and have fun with them!

ENDNOTES

1. Prizzi, E. and Hoffman, J.: *Interactive Bulletin Boards,* Carthage, Fearon, 1984, pp. 1–6.
2. Wankelmen, Willard F. and Wigg, Phil: *A Handbook of Arts and Crafts.* Dubuque, Wm. C. Brown, 1985, pp. 24–28.
3. Brisson, Lynn: 3-D Bulletin Boards, New York, Fantail, 1989, p. 8.
4. Ibid., pp. 7–8.

Chapter Eleven

LEARNING CENTERS

Ideas for Establishing and Managing Learning Centers in the Classroom.

You probably won't be ready to implement learning centers the first day of school, but somewhere around February you may be ready for the challenge.

Over the years, learning centers have gained the reputation of "total openness," having no structure and little direction. Critics say children are free to do as they please and make their own learning decisions. In reality, any teacher who has ever attempted implementing learning centers in their classroom, realizes the opposite is true. In order for learning centers to be successful, exact planning and organizational skills are required. Only then will the learning center be a productive learning experience.

What is a Learning Center?

A learning center has many characteristics and is not solely defined as a physical area for learning. A learning center is a technique designed with a purpose to enrich, to review, to reinforce or to teach some new skill or skills. It provides opportunities for children to work independently or in small groups to encourage divergent thinking. A learning center addresses the special needs of each child in a sequentially organized fashion which are not totally free, unstructured, nor are they inflexible. It can include activities that are concrete or abstract and are focused on the abilities and interests of the student. Lastly, a learning center is a place with multi-level activities, which can be teacher-made or commercially prepared and are chosen by the student or assigned by the teacher.[1]

Types of Learning Centers

A centering approach to learning can include the following types of centers: research, skills, listening, discovery, independent study, critical thinking, dramatics, games, observation/experimentation as well as blocks, housekeeping or cooking.

These centers can include such curriculum areas as: reading, math, language arts, writing, art, music, health science, social studies and/or science.

Steps in Developing a Learning Center

Your first step will be to decide the number of learning centers you would like to have and the curriculum areas that will be involved.

Next, arrange your room into areas and designate their specific use. For example a learning center that will require audio/visual materials will need to be located near an electrical outlet. If you have a science center you may want to place it near the window for conducting experiments with light.

The third step is a bit more complicated. You need to determine the purpose of each learning center and define each of the skills and concepts to be learned, enriched or reinforced.

It is a good idea to label the learning center both pictorially and numerically to identify their purpose and to motivate their use.

Try to provide materials and equipment that is creative, colorful and durable in order to construct an attractive center.

Now, all you need to do is to design a record keeping system and plan the actual management and routing of the centers.

Setting up Learning Centers

The first thing you must direct your attention to is the physical layout of the classroom. How will you group the desks? Where will you place the centers? Again, make yourself a little sketch or diagram of the room and where you'd like to put your learning centers. I've provided two such examples (Figures 4 and 5).

Next, think about movement within the room. Is there enough space to safely have organized movement? What will be the method of getting help and advice? Where will the children leave their completed work? How will it be returned to them? All of these figure into your movement plan.

Then you'll need to concentrate on Centering Rules and Honor System.

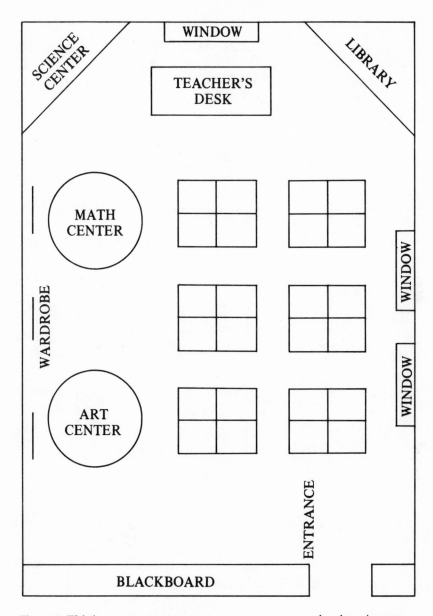

Figure 4. This is one way to arrange your room to accommodate learning centers.

Older children can develop their own rules which should focus on sharing, cooperation and behavior. Younger children may need to discuss rules and why they are important before you post and discuss centering rules.

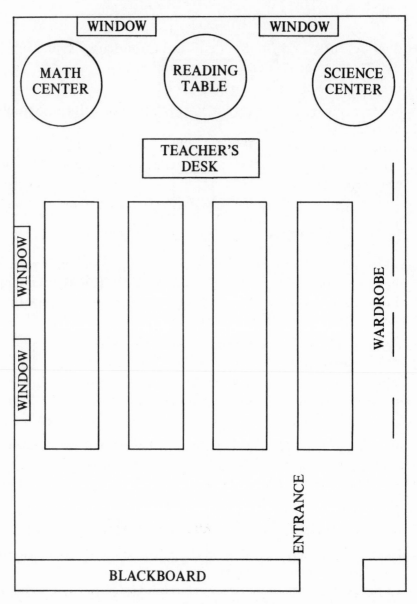

Figure 5. This is an alternative way to accommodate learning centers. Your desk is strategically placed in the center of all the action. It also requires the least amount of desk movement.

A short discussion on the Honor System can also help. Children will be using desks that belong to other students. You can discuss respecting others' property which includes desk contents.

Setting Up Groups

Teachers set up groups quite often during the school year. Here are some tips for grouping students for learning centers:

1. Mix boys with girls.
2. Separate any children who do not get along or will cause trouble.
3. Select a group leader.
4. Provide folders and evaluation sheets for each child.
5. Provide a chart of groups and locations for those who forget or were absent.

Scheduling System for Learning Centers

The amount of time spent in each learning center depends upon the individual needs of each child, curriculum requirements and the subject areas of the learning centers. There is no "right or wrong" in scheduling. One way is a rotation scheduling system.

1. Centers are created around the classroom.
2. Each student is assigned to a specific center at a specific time.
3. This system is most easily used when the class is divided into small groups of children (usually no more than six) who rotate around the different centers in a fixed pattern.

I find the rotational system a good one to use when you begin introducing learning centers in the classroom. It provides some structure to the learning center experience.

Tips for Successful Learning Centers

1. Centers can focus on any topic. Allow students to make some suggestions.
2. Children learn by touch and experimenting. Be sure to include lots of things to feel and explore.
3. Children learn from each other. They need time to interchange ideas and receive feedback from peers.
4. Children should be encouraged and guided to pursue the topic beyond the learning center activities, especially when great interest is shown.

5. Centers should integrate all subject areas to be totally effective as a learning tool.
6. Small group and large group activities also should be a part of the curriculum. Include stories, films, dramatizations and arts and crafts.
7. Remember not only to soak up students' enthusiastic comments, but also to stop and analyze your mistakes. Evaluation allows you to step back and find out what is working and what is not and then plan for tomorrow.
8. Be sure to build in a catch-up day for those students who are slower to complete their work, absent or pulled out for special services.[2]

Learning centers should be a product of you and your experiences with children. How often would you like to have centers in your room? Should your room be a "total center" room? Or a monthly center room? The choice is yours.

Portable Centers

Not everyone has the luxury of space or permanent learning centers or maybe you're not sure if learning centers are for you. Why not try a portable center? Here's how:

1. Any grocery store box wide enough to hold your planned activities will work nicely. Make sure it is long enough to hold a stationery store envelope (or whatever type you choose to use to store your activities). The box should be trimmed enough to conveniently fit in the storage area you designate.
2. Decorate the box. You can use colorful wrapping paper or contact paper. Use the same paper to cover the activity holders. This will help the children to clean up quickly and return any loose items to their proper place.
3. Each activity should be clearly numbered in the top right hand corner of the envelope. Additional material inside the envelope should also be numbered with corresponding numbers. For younger children, you can use dots above the written number. This will help to keep the activities in sequence.
4. A colorful contract can be made on a duplicating master and copies made on construction paper. Each child should have his/

her own contract for purposes of record keeping. As the child completes an activity, he/she may color in the number on his/her contract that corresponds to the number of the completed activity.

5. Task cards for the center should be laminated or covered with clear contact paper for durability. This will also allow the children to write with a greased pencil or watercolor pen directly on the cards. Then it can be washed off with a damp tissue. This saves time and paper.[3]

A viewing center can be set up as a semi permanent learning center. This center can be used with many different topics. Numerous excellent filmstrips are available at county education offices or right in your own library. The filmstrips can be shown at a reading table near an electrical outlet and projected into a grocery box. Paint or cover the box with black. Staple a white piece of paper on the inside bottom of the box. Turn the box on its side and provide ample filmstrip review worksheets and your center is complete. The kids think it is a treat to sit and watch a movie and their learning too. Who knows, maybe even one or two students may decide to become a film critic from this experience.

Painting centers work well with all age groups. Everyone loves to paint. Easels are ideal, but often they are few and far between. Cover several tables or a shelf area with newspaper and you are ready for art. Keep a large container of water (no glass jars, please) near the table for the children to wash their brushes. Painting smocks can be brought from home. Some children like to wear pretty smocks and others are content with an old shirt. I keep two or three in my closet. I've even worn an old shirt to save my clothes from the paint. The students can bring in newspapers and the paint should be easily accessible. If you hang a clothes line somewhere in your room and if each student brings a hanger and two clothes pins, you have a great way to display and dry their work. Try to hang the clothesline where your students can reach it without your help.

Many teachers like to keep animals in their classrooms. Some classroom favorites are: goldfish, turtles, frogs and gerbils. Animals can provide new learning experiences for your students in addition to learning about responsibility. Your class will have lots of questions, so do your homework. You can have them research the animal before it comes to school and learn to care for it. The librarian will be happy to help your students learn more about their class pet. One word of caution, before you decide to add a class pet to your room, get permission from your Supervisor.

Rita and Ken Dunn have done a great deal of work with learning styles and they suggest you try these learning stations:

Magic Carpet

This term is used to describe an area where children can escape from the noise and activity of the class to a quiet corner of the room. It is usually carpeted or there are several mats upon which to sit. No one may talk, students may relax, read silently or rest. The books in this area are only to be used by students in this area. Books are magical and what better place to read and enjoy them.

Game Table

Games can be an exciting way to learn. They can be set up in different sections of the classroom. When assignments are complete, students should be able to go quietly to the table and select a game. You can help them by coding them according to their difficulty.

Little Theater

At this center students are permitted to make slides, filmstrips, rolled paper movies, books, scrapbooks and many other educational project materials related to drama, creativity and production. These projects are related to the application, reinforcement or review of material they have learned.[4]

As you can see there are many ways to incorporate learning centers into your classroom. They are not easy. They require a great deal of thought and planning, but are certainly a valuable educational tool. Learning Centers can provide a productive learning experience for your students as well as a rewarding teaching experience for yourself.

Audio-Visual Equipment

Audio-visual equipment comes in all shapes and sizes and can add a new dimension to any lesson. Your mission, should you accept the challenge, is to become familiar with the scope of audio-visual equipment available and to learn how to use them wisely.

The first thing you should do, even before classes begin, is to find out what equipment is available for you to use. You can ask your colleagues, supervisor or school secretary. (You may want to note the proper lingo, a/v equipment or a/v aids are often used when referring to these machines.)

In some schools each classroom has their own equipment, but in other schools you'll need to borrow the equipment. Find out what forms are necessary for borrowing and how much notice is necessary. In one of my schools it was necessary to ask for a television set at least 2 days before it was needed. If you wanted the video camera or VCR the office needed 3–5 days notice.

Before discussing the various types of audio/visual equipment, here are a few helpful hints:

Make sure that the outlets in your classroom are working. This may sound silly, but it may just save your lesson. Teachers often use audio/visual equipment during an observation. The teachers often become quite flustered and embarrassed when the equipment fails. It is then very difficult to continue your lesson with the same excitement. Check that your outlets work and that the machine itself is working properly well before that observation.

Buy a two and three prong adapter and keep it in your desk drawer. Some of the equipment may have three prongs and your outlet or extension cord may only accept two prongs. By having a two and three prong adapter, you'll be ready for anything.

Be sure to get an extension cord with the audio/visual equipment. If not, beg or borrow an extension cord from a co-worker; extension cords are vitally important. Often outlets are in out of the way spots; an extension cord allows you to move the equipment to where you want it, rather than moving the children. This way everyone can see and participate.[5]

Tape Recorders and Tape Players

The most obvious uses for tape recorders are in conjunction with filmstrip or slide presentations. Tape players can be used in most subject areas. They can help to individualize learning. They can be used as part of a Learning Center or Listening Center. The recorder can serve one child wearing headphones or a small group of children sitting in a small circle or at a table. Why not try some of these ideas: tape missed lessons for absentees, extra credit assignments, student recordings of book reports, practice in following directions or to improve listening skills. Have several storybooks and tapes available for those children who would like to relax and listen to a story.

Filmstrip Projectors and Filmstrips

There are usually several of these floating around your school, as well as some terrific filmstrips. Filmstrips are available on just about every subject. Check with your co-worker as to their location. Very often the school librarian has a wealth of filmstrips you can borrow. Some filmstrips have a printed narrative, others are accompanied by an audio tape. Little "beeps" on the tape indicate that the filmstrip should be advanced to the next frame. It is important to pay attention and to see that the filmstrip and tape are coordinated.

Some schools are fortunate enough to own an "all in one" filmstrip player. This type of machine is best used in a learning center. It does not require a screen. It looks like a television set and projects the picture on to its own screen.

Slide Projector

Slide projectors are great. With slides the teacher controls the rate and provides the narration. I used many of my own slides for presentations. For example, when we studied volcanos, I brought my slides from Hawaii's Volcano National Park. They provided the motivation for my lesson. You can also use slides as scenery for a class play or use slides in a Learning Center to introduce a new area of study. Be sure to use the remote and move around during a slide presentation. When the lights go out anything can happen. When you walk around, it lets your students know that you are still in control of the lesson.[6]

Television and Radio

Listening to a radio program or watching a television show can introduce multimedia to your class. They have these things in their own homes, yet you can show them the educational value they have.

Listening to a radio program is a real challenge because children are so accustomed to a visual presentation. You may need to teach or at least review listening skills. Give them several things to listen for and have them write the answers down. This helps their concentration when no visual stimulation is present.

For worthwhile programs on radio, you can check local papers or with your local Board of Education. They often sponsor educational radio programs. Some of my favorites included: mysteries, famous biographies and sing-a-longs.

Television can be an excellent learning tool. There are many educational programs on the Public Broadcasting Stations in your area. Many of them tie in nicely with the curriculum. Again, the Board of Education may have an educational channel you can receive right in your classroom. Check with your school office for a guide to these programs.

I often use television to follow current event stories: Inaugurations, Press Conferences and Shuttle Launches. I was scheduled to have my class watch the Challenger Space Shuttle launch, but due to a mix-up, we never received the television set on time. In this instance, I was thankful for the mix-up. We did see the accident later on and we followed that story for months to come.

Television reception isn't always the greatest, so before using the television, check it out. Try it in several spots in your classroom until you can get the best reception.

Movie Projectors

Schools usually have one or two projectors. They are used mostly during school assembly programs. Films are available from many large companies. Be sure to preview any materials you receive to be sure they are worthwhile, age appropriate and can hold the student's attention. (Most movie projectors are being retired now that video tapes and recorders are readily available.)

Video Cameras, Video Recorders and Video Tapes

If your school has this type of equipment, the possibilities are endless. Your students can become real camera buffs and learn a great deal about filming from using a Video Camera. You can tape a lesson, class trip or even a class performance. The children love to see themselves and will become instant movie stars, directors and producers.

If your school has a video recorder, you can tape educational programs and bring them into class to share. There are many educational video tapes, classic plays and novels, in addition to Sesame Street type video tapes. Choose and use them wisely. Your school may even have a video tape library. Parents often volunteer to tape programs at home for classroom use and they become a part of the school video library. I wouldn't go out and purchase a tape unless you can use that tape several times. I check with my local library first. You can borrow the tape and use it in school the next day.

Overhead Projectors

Overhead projectors are versatile and simple to operate. They allow the teacher to face the students, while presenting the lesson in an interesting manner. Overhead projectors use commercially printed transparencies which you can mark with colorful, grease pencils. You can use two or more transparencies over the other. This one transparency over another comes in handy when you are building a lesson. The first transparency may have several blanks to be filled in and the second transparency may contain the answers.

If your school owns a thermofax machine you can create your own transparency and a duplicating master at the same time. Check with the school office to see if this type of machine is available and how to use it. If you do not know how to operate any type of machinery, please do not be afraid to ask. The equipment is often very expensive to fix and replace. Do not be afraid of looking silly or foolish. Not all equipment is the same. Ask questions.

When you are working with the overhead projector, do not reveal the entire transparency at once. Cover the lesson and move down the page as you present each point. Also do not tie yourself to the machine, move about the room as in any lesson.[7]

Screens

Projectors require a screen of some sort. Some teachers are lucky enough to have a screen above the blackboard. Others must rely on a collapsible tripod based screen. If these options are not available to you try using a window shade in your room or the back or a large pull down map. You can also bring an old sheet or table cloth from home.

Record Player

As far as I know, record players are not yet obsolete. Many recordings can now be found on compact disc, but there are not too many schools who own such equipment yet. Music has always been a part of my classroom. The children love to sing along with children's songs and it is relaxing to listen to while creating an art project. I've also used them as music for some class plays. If you do not play the piano or have one in your classroom, this is one way to bring music to your class. One word of caution, be sure the needle works and that you have selected the correct speed for the recording. There's nothing that will set the tone of a lesson faster than a record played at the wrong speed.

Duplicating and Copy Machines

The duplicating or ditto machine makes copies of teacher-made tests, quizzes or worksheets. Many of the "basal" reading series come with master worksheets to reinforce reading skills. Get to know the duplicating machines, learn how to use them and how to make your own masters.

Last, but not least, is the copying machine. Many schools have copying machines, but limit the use of them. The paper and maintenance is costly, so find out what the restrictions are and use them wisely.

Before you use any audio/visual equipment in front of a class, try it out. I know I keep repeating this message, but it is important to note. Materials to be viewed or listened to should also be checked just prior to use. Very often an audio tape gets tangled or filmstrips are scratched. The best defense is to check them and make a dry run. It is also in your best interest to have another activity planned should your school lose power or the equipment fails at the last second. Sometimes it is a simple bulb that blew out the minute you hit the on switch. Just be prepared for anything.

When you are responsible for storing audio/visual equipment in your classroom, do so carefully. If something gets broken the ultimate responsibility is yours. Wrap all cords and store the machines on a safe shelf in a closet that locks. That will prevent an accident of a different kind.

Each school has someone in charge of all the audio/visual equipment. Be sure to inform this person when a machine doesn't work properly. If all the teachers do this, the machines can be repaired and will be in excellent shape when you need them.

Computers

Test your knowledge.

True or False   RAM stands for Random Access Memory.

True or False   A computer program is a form of software.

True or False   A keyboard is an example of computer hardware.

True or False   An error in a computer program is called a "bug."[8]

(Answer key: True, True, True, True)

There is no denying computers are very much a part of our lives, both inside and outside the classroom. A computer can be a teacher's best friend. It can help you keep records, average grades and write reports. It can help provide instruction to your students while releasing you to interact more personally with other students.

Keep in mind that a computer is just another device to help you do your job.

Here are some tips to help you get started:

1. Learn to use the computer yourself. Have someone show you all the features and how everything works.
2. Use the computer for your own purposes; writing letters, averaging grades, creating and updating handouts and tests.
3. Peruse the available software. Become familiar with it, use it and play with it. This will build your confidence and you'll be ready to help your students when they have a problem.
4. Keep in mind that a computer is a tool for learning, not an isolated activity. Use it as a means to an end.
5. Do "real things" with a computer. Create real letters and real assignments. Don't get tied up with making the activities fun.

Help to show your students the importance of computers outside the classroom.

6. Don't devote all your time to teaching how to use a word processor, but how to use that word processor to read or write should be stressed.

7. Don't be fooled by the "student high interest" in computers. Excitement about an activity doesn't necessarily mean it is effective.[9]

Creative uses of a variety of media will increase the probability that your students will learn more and even retain more information from your lessons. In addition, your students will be getting a different kind of education, a media education: how to set up and operate the various types of audio/visual equipment. Two good reasons to use audio/visual equipment in your classroom.

ENDNOTES

1. Collinwood, Gerry: *Ideas for Learning Centers. Third and Fourth Grade.* Handsford, Kings County Curriculum Services, p. 4. 1977.
2. Ibid. pp. 6–9.
3. Klawetter, Pamela: "Minicenters," *Instructor,* V 90, pp. 64–71. September, 1980.
4. Dunn, Rita and Dunn, Kenneth: *Teaching Students Through Their Individual Learning Styles: A Practical Approach.* Reston, pp. 34–53. 1978.
5. Brown, James, Lewis, Richard and Harcleroad, Fred: *A V Instruction, Technology, Media and Methods.* New York, McGraw Hill, pp. 167–168. 1977.
6. Alexander, Carole: Staff Development Workshop "Presentation Skills." Massapequa Union Free School District, Nassau County, 1991.
7. Brown op. cit., pp. 417–424.
8. Community School District 24, Staff Development Workshop, "Computer Education," Queens, New York p. 1. 1984.
9. Dockterman, David and Bowman, Sally: "Why We Should Do "Real Things" With Computers." *American Teacher,* V 74 p. 2. December, 1989–January, 1990.

Chapter Twelve

DESIGNING INSTRUCTIONAL MATERIALS

Name Three Types of Instructional Materials

If you can cut, paste, print legibly and apply contact paper, you can design and create instructional materials for your classroom.

Instructional materials come in all shapes and sizes. Story starters, learning circles, task cards, geoboards, activity cards, scramble boards, sequence cards, puzzles and games are all examples of instructional materials.

Instructional materials are particularly appealing to those students who find it difficult to sit still for periods of time. They are also a boon to teachers who want to individualize instruction, but cannot do so because the needs and problems of the students are too diverse.

Teacher made instructional materials are inexpensive, easy to make, and durable. More importantly they can meet the needs of learners who are at different academic levels. I was fortunate enough to inherit a classroom full of teacher made instructional materials and they really helped me bridge some gaps during that first year.

Grab your scissors, paste and markers and let's get started.

Story Starters

Story starters are great for children who enjoy writing stories, but never seem to know what to write about.

Materials

old magazines	scissors
construction paper	paste or glue
clear contact paper	markers

Directions

Magazine pictures make great story starters. Thumb through some old magazines, cut out pictures that you find appealing. Paste or glue each picture to a colorful piece of construction paper. Write three or four interesting questions under the picture, then cover both sides of the paper with clear contact. You can rubberband the pictures together or you can cut a cereal box in half, cover it with some colorful paper. Cover the box with clear contact and label the box, Story Starters, and display it where your students will notice. You'll be pleased with all the stories that will find their way to your desk. Instead of questions you may want to write the first two paragraphs of the story and ask them to finish the story using the picture as a guide.

Learning Circles

A learning circle is a fun way for children to review many skills. You can use them to review basic math facts, spelling words, historical data, even science vocabulary.

Materials

two pieces of heavy construction paper
one wire coat hanger
colorful markers
scissors
strong adhesive glue
eight colored plastic clip-on clothespins
clear contact paper
pencil
ruler

Directions

Cut two circles about eighteen inches in diameter. Divide each circle into eight equal sections. In each of the eight sections, place a picture of the word you would like your students' to spell or recognize. Example, ball, bat, and glove. Print the word that matches the picture on the tip end of a clothespin. Do the same for the rest of the sections and clothespins. Turn the second circle around so the eight sections become the back. Print the word again on this second circle in the appropriate section, opposite the picture. Cover both circles separately with the clear contact paper. Place the wire hanger between the two circles and fasten them together with your glue. It is somewhat easier if you bend the hanger into a circle shape before gluing. Your self correcting learning circle is now ready to use. Place the clothespins in a small plastic bag and attach it to the hanger. The children who wish to use this circle will remove the clothespins and match the pictures to the words on the clothespins. When all eight are complete, they can check their work by turning the circle around to see if they correctly matched the words. The words on the clothespins should match the words on the back side of the circle.[1] These circles conveniently hang just about anywhere.

Task Cards

Task cards are usually designed in sets of eight. Each set teaches facts on one specific concept. They are usually self correcting and are used by one student at a time.

Materials

colored oaktag or cardboard	markers
scissors	clear contact
pencil	ruler
directions	

Begin by listing exactly what you want your students to learn about a topic. Let's use map skills as an example. Here are some map skill terms:

ocean	island	continent
bay	isthmus	latitude
inlet	longitude	

Cut the colored oaktag into eight rectangles each three by eight inches. On the left side of each rectangle, print one of the words on your list. On the right side of each rectangle print the definition of the word. Cover each rectangle with clear contact. Cut each rectangle into two parts using different designs to separate each. Place each set in a colorful envelope and place the envelopes in a box and label it Task Cards. A child can then take a folder to his/her seat and empty the contents. They can match each word and definition. They'll know they are correct because the design you cut will match only for the two correct pieces.

island	a piece of land completely surrounded by water
continent	one of seven large divisions of land on earth

Geoboards

This is an excellent tool for teaching concepts of shape, sets, angles, measurement and number patterns.

Materials

light weight wood less than ½" thick	rubber bands
small nails	small saw
sand paper	hammer
ruler	ruler
pencil	

Directions

Cut the wood into six by six inch squares. Sand and smooth the edges with the sandpaper. Paint if desired. Measure every three centimeters and hammer in a small nail, there will be six nails in each row. Give the geoboards to several students along with several rubberbands and see what they can discover by stretching the rubberbands between nailheads. Children often try to shoot the rubber bands. Let them know that this will not be tolerated and that they will be held accountable for each rubber band.

Activity Cards

Activity cards are short, interesting and creative assignments. Usually found in sets of ten cards and can be used in all academic areas. Begin by developing cards that draw upon existing knowledge and build to more advanced levels of understanding.

Materials

construction paper or index cards	stickers
scissors	markers
grease pencils or water soluble pens	contact paper
ruler	pencil

Directions

Cut ten three by five inch cards from construction paper. (Index cards can be used, but they are not as colorful.) Decide what skill you would like to focus on: capitalization, vowels, thinking skills, sequence, feelings or vocabulary are some areas you may want to consider. Write a set of directions at the top of each card and give one example of what the child should do. Give five or six questions for the student to answer, leaving enough space for the child to write his/her answer. Using markers or stickers decorate the card. Write the answers on the other side of the card. Cover each card, both sides with clear contact. Store the cards in a small box with an appropriate title. Here's what an activity card might look like:

Directions

Circle each letter that should be capitalized.
Remember to capitalize holidays, months of the year and days of the week.
ex. 1. mary went to school on monday.

1. january is the first month of the year.
2. in february we celebrate valentine's day.
3. this year christmas falls on saturday.

You would add several more sentences and the students would use their greased pencils to circle their answers and then they can check their answers on the back, erase them with a damp cloth and move onto another activity card.

Scramble Board

A unique way to learn vocabulary or other important information. Children match the word with its definition, a question with an answer, problem with solution or parts of sentences.

Materials

one piece of light weight wood less than ½" thick
white paper   sandpaper
small saw   small nails
hammer   markers
rubber bands   glue
ruler   pencil

Directions

Cut the piece of wood with your saw into a piece which is 8½" by 11", sand and paint, if desired. Decide what is to be learned by your students and outline the questions and answers. Write the directions, questions and answers on a piece of paper, approximately 7½″ by 10″. Glue this paper to one side of the wood. On a second sheet of paper the same size write the answers and the questions properly matched. Glue this paper to the other side of the wood. Hammer in nails on side one after each question and before each answer. Stretch rubber bands from one nail to the other straight across. Your students will remove the rubber bands and use them to correctly match each question and answer. Then they will flip the board over and check their work on the back. They will return the rubber bands to their original position so that another student may use it.[2] Here's an example:

Math Scramble

addend *	* a number to be divided
sum *	* a number added to another number
dividend *	* an answer to a problem in division
quotient *	* the total of two or more numbers

Sequence Cards

Children organize events and objects into a logical sequence. Sequence cards are great for developing logical thinking, memory and communication skills.

Materials

construction paper   glue or paste
pictures, photos or old books   contact paper
scissors

Directions

Cut the construction paper into three inch by three inch squares. You will need four for each sequence. Sequences can be as simple as steps in brushing your teeth or planting a seed. More involved sequences could include: how to build a snowman or how to bowl. Cut pictures from old childrens' magazines, photographs or old story books. Paste each picture onto a square. Write a small number or letter on the back to indicate its proper order. Cover the entire square with clear contact paper. Keep each sequence set in a small envelope with a title. Put all the envelopes into a box and label it Sequence Cards.

Puzzles

Puzzles are not only fun, but educational too. They strengthen eye hand coordination, perception of shape and size, as well as visual discrimination skills.

Materials

cardboard   colorful magazine pictures
glue   scissors
clear contact paper

Directions

Find a picture to use as a puzzle. Your Backyard and Ranger Rick have wonderful animal pictures to use. Numbers and letters, even a picture of a clock can make a great puzzle. Paste the picture to thin cardboard the same size as the picture. Next decide how many pieces you would like this puzzle to have. Remember younger children need fewer pieces and older children like the challenge of many pieces. Use the back of the puzzle to design the various shapes and outline the shapes in pencil. Place an identifying mark on each piece of the puzzle. You can use a number or letter. This helps for sorting later. Cover the entire piece of cardboard with clear contact paper. Cut out the pieces. Store the pieces in a small coffee can, which has been cleaned and covered. Store on a convenient shelf.

Games

Some teachers feel that games do not belong in the classroom. In my room the game shelf was quite popular. Games have many purposes by providing:

1. an alternative teaching method
2. small group interaction
3. a relaxing and fun way to learn

Games also stimulate a child's intellectual abilities:

1. the ability to analyze problems
2. the ability to synthesize
3. memory
4. convergent and divergent thinking.[3]

Board games can be store bought or created by you. Two easy games to begin with are Bingo and Lotto. Bingo and Lotto are very versatile, they adapt easily to age level and subject matter. Both games provide a fun way to review previously taught material.

Bingo

Materials

oaktag or cardboard	pencil
scissors	markers
bingo markers or construction paper	clear contact paper
	ruler

Directions

Cut the oaktag paper into several five inch by five inch squares. If possible, create one square for each child in your class. Divide each square into twenty-five one inch boxes. If you have younger children you may want larger and fewer boxes. Decide what type of Bingo game you would like to design: color, number, word recognition, alphabet letters or multiplication products. Mark the center box with the word Free. Then assign each box a number, letter or word depending on the type of game. Cover each card with clear contact. Purchase bingo markers or make markers by cutting construction paper into small squares. Store in a large envelope or pocketed folder. Chips can be stored in a zip lock type pencil case.

Lotto

Lotto is a great game for the younger children. Some of my slower readers enjoyed playing word lotto and managed to learn some new vocabulary words in the process.

Materials

oaktag	paste
magazine pictures	markers
clear contact	pencil
ruler	

Directions

Cut the oaktag into several six inch by six inch squares. Divide each square into nine two inch squares. Select pictures, cut and paste each picture in one of your two inch squares. Cover the entire board with clear contact paper. Divide another piece of oaktag into nine two inch by two inch boxes. Print one word on each card to match the pictures. Cover the card with, you guessed it, clear contact paper. (I should own stock I use so much clear contact!) Cut each square and store all pieces in a decorative envelope.

You can purchase gameboards and pieces at the Teacher's Store. They sell books of game boards, dice, spinners, markers and tokens. The possibilities are endless.

You can also purchase commercially produced games for your classroom. These too can be found in the Teacher's Store. You can also purchase games from any local toy store. Some favorites include:

Checkers	Boggle	S'Math
Chess	Quizmo	Yatzee
Dominoes	Clue	Trouble
Sorry	Flash Cards	Connect Four

You do not have to purchase these games, your students can bring them in on a designated day. You can ask for donations, often the children throw games out because pieces are missing. You can purchase replacement pieces and recycle the game. Yard sales are also a great place to shop for games.

Class Games

Children love to play class games. They think they're playing and wasting learning time, but you know they are learning.

Spelling Bees

Spelling Bees are always a challenge. Everyone gets to participate and move around a little bit. You can begin with the weeks spelling words, throw in some "old" spelling words for review, then onto the "new" and difficult words. I usually give my class some notice that a "bee" is in their future. For a change of pace, I have Math Bees which review basic math facts. Depending on the grade level you can have an addition, subtraction, multiplication or division bee. I also have Science Bees with scientific vocabulary words. The students can spell the words and gain an extra point for their team if they can explain or define the word. I often pit the boys against the girls, but to be different I mix the groups and the winners do not have to do the homework in that subject area that night. If you win the Spelling Bee, you receive a certificate which entitles you to one night of no spelling homework!

Spelling Baseball

Spelling baseball is also quite popular. You divide the class into two teams. Two teams alternate. The hitter on the up-at-bat team must spell the word the "pitcher" on the other team asks them to spell from a given list. If he does, he may go to first base, if not, he is out. After three outs the other team is up at bat. Each member of the "up" team forces one another around the bases and a run scores when players are forced home. You can decide how many innings to play before the game starts.

Alphabet Game

Recommended for third grade and up. The class is divided into two teams. The teams line up on opposite sides of the classroom, facing each other. Each child is given two letters of the alphabet on cards to hold. You'll need one of every letter and extra vowels and consonants. You can determine which extra letters you'll need from your spelling word list. The teacher calls out a word and the children who are holding the letters in that word must move in front of their team and arrange themselves so the word is spelled correctly. The first team to do this gets the point. The team with the most points wins.

Hangman

Everyone likes to play hangman. It is a great way to review spelling words or even vocabulary words. Use the blackboard, set up the hanging post and leave the rest to the class. You can give them the words to use. The object is to guess the word before the little man gets "hung." I do not allow the children to shout out letters or the answer. You must raise your hand to be a winner.

Sudden Death

Sudden death is a math game played at the blackboard. Select five children and ask them to stand outside the classroom door or with their backs to the blackboard. Write the same math problem in five different spots on the blackboard. Make sure each child has a piece of chalk. Ask each child to stand in front of a math problem. When you give the signal to start, the five children work through the math problem. The first child to finish with the correct answer wins that round. Continue with rounds of five children until everyone has had a turn. Give a new problem to each group of five children. All the "winners" enter "sudden death" the final round. Make this problem a challenging one. Your class will ask to play this game again and again. I excuse the winner of sudden death from that night's math assignment.

Concentration

This game relies on the child's memory. Concentration can be played with math facts, antonyms, synonyms and homonyms and other similar material. Here's what to do: Make up twenty index cards with antonyms written on them. Tape them face down on the blackboard. Divide the class into two teams. Each child gets a chance to turn over two cards. If they match (opposites in this case; hot and cold, up and down) their team gets a point. No match then the cards must be turned over again and no point is scored.

These are only a few of many learning games that you can share with your class. For more ideas check your curriculum guides and children's game books available at your library. These games involve physical activity, getting out of your seat and moving around. Children need plenty of physical activity.

Physical activity is not the same as physical education or athletics.

Anyone who has watched children knows they need to move about. It is the rare child or adult who can sit still and concentrate for hours at a time. Therefore, it is important to plan breaks in your day where children can move about and have some physical activity. Research has shown that moderate exercise helps learning.[4] Children performed better in addition tasks after moderate exercise. Classroom activities can be quite simple—marching around the classroom, stretching exercises, shaking out their limbs, Simon Says, Hokey Pokey, or Head, Shoulders, Knees and Toes. These activities do not require equipment and can be done inside the classroom.

If you have the opportunity to use the gym, basement, or outdoor yard, give your class a twenty minute treat. Here are a few ideas.

Younger Children Like Circle Games:

Farmer in the Dell
Did You Ever See a Lassie
Looby Loo
Duck, Duck, Goose
Follow the Leader
Bone, Bone Who's Got the Bone

Older Children Enjoy More Challenging Games:

Freezer Tag
Relay Races
Kickball
Red Rover
Steal the Bacon

Instructions for these games can be found in most children's game books.[5] You can ask the school librarian for help locating books. You can also check with the physical education instructor for more physical activities.

A Final Thought on Instructional Materials and Games

As a new teacher you probably will not be ready to design instructional materials until mid way through the year. Don't forget that older students and parents are wonderful resources. If you provide a sample, they can duplicate and create additional materials. Yes, it is probably easier to purchase these materials, but they will not focus on the topics or objectives you need to teach.

Instructional materials and games provide new teaching methods; they make children aware of their own academic growth and help to build a positive self-image. Try them and see.

ENDNOTES

1. Dunn, Rita and Dunn, Ken: *Teaching Students Through Their Individual Learning Styles: A Practical Approach.* Reston, pp. 319–322. 1978.
2. Ibid. p. 271.
3. Guilford, J. P.: *Intelligence, Creativity, and Their Educational Implications.* San Diego, Knapp, 1968.
4. Ibid.
5. Kamiya, Arthur: *Elementary Teachers Handbook of Outdoor Games.* New York, Parker, 1985.

Chapter Thirteen

TESTING: A PRACTICAL GUIDE

Let's see how well you do on this quick quiz.

Fill in the blank.

1. All tests should be made to _____ specific learning.
2. Students _____ to be taught how to take tests.
3. Before a large test you should provide the students with a _____.
4. Standardized tests use the same _____ to measure student performance.
5. A short test is called a _____.

(Answer key: 1. evaluate, 2. need, 3. review, 4. standard, 5. quiz.)

Test is a loaded word. The mere mention of the word makes us a bit apprehensive.

Tests are important, especially to school children. A test can measure a basic skill, or it can measure the child's ability to learn. Tests can affect a child's grade placement as well. We are a testing society. We test children entering school, while in school, before they graduate, to get into college and to get certain jobs. Tests are helpful to educators; they help us to measure and evaluate and improve education.

There are two basic types of tests you will be concerned with: those that are teacher-made and those that are standardized.

Standardized Testing

Sometime during the year, you will be required to give a standardized test. A standardized test uses the same standard to measure student performance across the country. Everyone takes the same test according to the same rules. This makes it possible to measure each student's performance against that of others. The group with whom a student's progress is compared is a "norm group" and consists of many students of the same age or grade who took the same test.[1]

You will recognize standardized tests because they always come with a student booklet and a teacher's instruction booklet. The older children (Grades 3 and up) receive a separate answer sheet as well. Younger children place their answers right in the booklet.

You can prepare yourself for this test by reading the teacher's instruction booklet along with a student booklet. Often, the supervisor will give you the instruction booklet a day or two in advance of the test. The children's booklet cannot be given to you until right before the test. Read the instructions carefully. Each section may repeat similar directions, but may ask the student in one section to pick the best answer, then in the next section ask them to select the one answer that does not belong. Also some tests require you to dictate to your class. Be sure to speak clearly and loudly.

Check to see if any other supplies are necessary. For example, #2 pencils are needed for these tests; be sure to have extras on hand and erasers too! For the math sections the students may need scrap paper. These tests are timed so be sure you have a stop watch or a watch with a second hand.

Walk around during the test and check to see that each child has marked their answers properly. These tests are scored by computers, the answers must be filled in with a #2 soft lead pencil. Each circle must be filled in entirely and with dark lead marks. If a child changes an answer, it must be erased completely before filling in the correct answer. There should be no stray pencil marks on the answer sheet and the sheet must not be folded or torn.

The question I'm asked most often by teachers is: "What is the difference between an aptitude and an achievement test?"

Aptitude refers to the ability to do school work. There are different tests to test a student's ability in various academic areas: math, reading, language arts, or science. Simply stated, aptitude measures what a child has the ability to do.

Achievement refers to the level of a student's skills and knowledge in specific academic areas, such as: listening, reading comprehension, vocabulary, computation, or problem solving. Simply, achievement measures what the child is actually doing.

Another type of test that has come into wide use throughout the country in recent years is called Competency Testing. These are criterion referenced tests. Students must get a certain score in order to "pass" the test. Criterion referenced tests have standards which are set up in advance to measure performance. An example would be a ten question computation test where every student with seven or more right answers would "pass." These tests are designed to show whether students have reached a particular level of skill or knowledge in a subject area, and are developed at the state or local level, not "standardized" nationally. These tests are given before promotion or graduation to the next level of education.[2]

New teachers in particular worry about these standardized tests. They believe the familiar saying: "tests measure the teacher as well as the students." Tests are one way of measuring what your students know, some students come to your class knowing more and will score better, others will not. This is no reflection on the teacher, as long as you are doing your best, you have nothing to fear. Still, new teachers ask me how to prepare their students for these standardized tests.

Students need to know how to take a test. There are many different materials available to teach students test-taking skills, but before you begin check with your supervisor to see what the policy is and if they supply the materials for you to use with your students. If your school does not supply these materials, they can be purchased from your local Teacher's Store. These duplicating materials provide exercises much like those found on standardized tests and provide plenty of drill and practice. (They even provide a practical answer grid.) Knowing how to take tests and what kind of questions will be asked eases the students' apprehensions and builds their confidence in test taking. We can all use more confidence when it comes to test taking.

Preparing Teacher-Made Tests

You CAN prepare good classroom tests. All it takes is a little knowledge and lots of practice. Many teachers, including myself, enter the classroom with little or no experience preparing tests. For the first few months of teaching, I relied on test items supplied by the textbook publisher. Much to my dismay these test items did not reflect the material covered in my classroom discussions. When even my brightest students performed poorly on my exams, I knew something was very wrong. My colleague pointed out that my test items were incompatible with my instructional objectives. I needed some direction and lots of help. Here are some guidelines that I found helpful.

Guidelines for Preparing Teacher-Made Tests

First, content should closely match what you do and what you require your students to do. Review your notes, assignments and textbook materials and outline the content that your test will cover.

Next, use your instructional objectives or teaching aims to help you identify potential test items. Good instructional objectives help us to focus on important learning experiences and thus are a good evaluative tool.

Now you must decide what levels of thinking (Bloom's Taxonomy) you want to test. Are you testing basic knowledge, or higher levels of thinking such as application and evaluation? How many questions will be on your test? How many at each level of thinking? How many points for each question? Will questions with higher level thinking skills be worth more? What type of written directions will be necessary? Once you can answer these questions you are ready to begin writing your test items.[3]

Guidelines for Writing Test Items

When writing test items, here are some things to remember:

1. Keep the reading level simple. (Unless you are testing vocabulary or comprehension skills.)
2. Arrange the items randomly, rather than the order presented during instruction.
3. Make your test items independent. Knowing the answer to one question should not depend on knowing the answer to the next.
4. Write unambiguous questions.
5. Use all levels of thinking skills on the test; do not rely on simple memory.
6. Use language appropriately; stay away from textbook jargon.
7. Make sure your test items do in fact test the objectives you have taught.[4]

There are many different types of teacher-made tests. The rest of this chapter will address each kind. I've tried to compile a short list of hints for each type of test to guide you.

True—False Test Items

True or False   George Washington was the First President of the
                  United States.

True—False tests have two advantages: they provide a simple and
direct way to measure student achievement and they are efficient. True—
False items can sample much of what a student has learned and are
particularly useful when used with films, maps, diagrams and graphs.

When writing true—false items try to:

1. Base each item on one important idea.
2. Be concise. Keep the item brief and right to the point.
3. Write clearly true or clearly false items.
4. Make your true and false items equal in length.
5. State all items positively.
6. Avoid clear cut patterns. (T,T. F,F,T,T,)[5]

Multiple Choice Test Items

Columbus discovered America in the Year _____.

    a. 1992
    b. 1817
    c. 1429
    d. 1492

Multiple choice items are widely used in standardized testing because
it provides an excellent means to test levels of academic achievement or
aptitude.

The multiple choice question usually consists of an incomplete declarative sentence, called the stem, and is followed by three to five possible
choices, only one is correct or clearly the best answer to the stem.

When writing multiple choice items here are some points to remember:

1. Clearly state the problem in the stem.
2. State item stems clearly and positively.
3. The stem can be an incomplete declarative sentence or a complete
   question.
4. The item should not have more than one acceptable answer.
5. The choices in an item should come at or near the end of the
   statement.
6. Order response options either numerically or alphabetically.

7. Use "all of the above" or "none of the above" as a choice only occasionally as a variation from the usual pattern.[6]

Matching Test Items

Father of our country	Ben Franklin
Discovered electricity	George Washington
Invented the telephone	Thomas Edison

Matching tests are designed to prompt students to see relationships between a set of items. A matching test consists of two columns: one set on the left the other on the right. Students are asked to match items in the two columns. They are, however, less suited for measuring higher levels of performance.

Here are a few guidelines for writing matching test items:

1. Use only homogeneous materials. For example, important events in history, prominent figures in history.
2. Place longer material in left hand corner.
3. Keep columns short. No more than ten or twelve items.
4. Directions for matching items should indicate: the basis for matching or relationship, the method of indicating answers, and whether the same choice or term can be used more than once.[7]

Completion Test Items

Abraham Lincoln was the _____ President of the United States.

Another name for this test is "fill in the blank test." Completion tests ask students to supply a number, word or phrase in the blank. Completion items are particularly helpful to early elementary teachers who are testing vocabulary, math or science skills. This too is a test which is most suited to low level thinking. Completion items are easy to write, here are a few tips:

1. Place blanks near the end of the statement.
2. Use single words or short phrases for the blanks; these can be scored more objectively than longer responses.
3. Prepare an answer key with all acceptable answers for each item.
4. Limit the number of blanks to one or two per item.

5. With early elementary school students, you may want to include an answer box from which students can select their answers.[8]

Essay Questions

Compare and contrast at least three different teacher made tests.

The last type of question is the essay question. Essay questions ask students to supply written answers to questions. Judgements are made about the accuracy and quality of the answer. There are two major drawbacks with essay tests: essay questions tap a smaller sample of student achievement and scoring essays are inconsistent. Essay items can be used to assess higher levels of thinking. Therefore:

1. Use words such as: compare, contrast, defend, argue or hypothesize in your essay question.
2. Prepare enough questions to sample the learning of the students adequately.
3. Prepare model answers before administering the exam.
4. The value and weight of each question should be indicated.
5. Give all students the same questions and allow enough time to give a complete answer. Each question shouldn't take more than 15 minutes.
6. Errors in spelling, grammar and usage should be corrected, but should not affect the student's grade.[9]

Here are a few tips for scoring essays more objectively:

1. Use your model answers as a guide.
2. Score the same question on all test papers before scoring the next question.
3. Read each essay twice before scoring, you sometimes miss things the first time around. It is sometimes helpful to put them away for a day and then go back and re-read them.
4. Try to cover the students' names for more objectivity.[10]

Testing is a fact of life for teachers, there are many different types of tests you can give your class during the course of the school year.

A Quiz

A quiz is shorter than an exam. This can be an oral or written quiz. Students can mark their own papers or switch papers with another student for grading. A quiz asks students to recall material that was just taught. This type of test is a great review and helps the teacher to refocus her lesson if need be.

The Weekly Test

The weekly test has become an institution. Remember the weekly spelling test, it still exists in most classrooms. Whether or not it will be present in your room is up to you. Weekly tests provide a good check for teachers on student progress. A good test will probably occur every ten days or so; this assures that you have covered enough material to test. There should be twenty to twenty-five test items because this number divides easily into one hundred. If you're thinking ahead, have this test duplicated and provide your students with an answer sheet. You can speed up grading and save the test papers for next year.

The Unit Test

A unit is usually a great deal of material to teach and you'll definitely want to test learning after a unit of work. This test will be longer than your weekly tests, approximately twenty-five to fifty questions. A unit test will have several parts. You will want to include all levels of thinking, and you will probably include a short essay. Again, a standard answer sheet will save time.

Midterms and Final Exams

These tests are inevitable! They are used more widely in late elementary and secondary schools. They are given in all subject areas. Don't panic! It is not as difficult as it sounds. First, decide what should have been learned during the year. You can check your goals for this information. Next, devise the different types of questions that will be used. Try to vary the types of questions, as well as their level. Assign importance to each part in terms of percentage and then calculate their worth in points. Students always like to know the point value of the questions. After the questions are written, write the directions for each section. Construct your answer sheet to go with the test and finally make up the answer key. Last read through your test carefully to eliminate any flaws. I sometimes go through my old exams and use questions from these exams on my midterms and finals. The students enjoy finding a question or two they remember from a previous test.

Other Test-Wise Tips

1. You should teach your students how to study. You can provide review sheets, or guide them in developing their own review materials.
2. You should teach your students how to read and follow directions carefully.
3. Prepare your students for tests. Let them know what kind of test it will be, what type of information will be covered and what will be necessary to bring to the test. (pens, pencils, calculators, or rulers.)
4. Explain why you are testing them on this material. This sometimes takes away some test anxiety.

Before a Test

1. Be sure the room is comfortable.
2. Be sure there is enough room. Move students around if necessary. This also controls "eyes that stray."
3. Explain procedures for cheating, fire drills, and using the bathroom.
4. Be sure they understand the directions and know to raise their hand for help, not get out of their seat.
5. What will they do if they finish early? Recheck, sit quietly, read a book? Will you collect their papers as they finish? As a class?

When you are sure there are no questions hand out the tests and answer sheets as quickly and efficiently as possible. This cuts down on anxiety.

During the test, walk around the room quietly. Stand and watch the students: Are they progressing according to the directions, are they having difficulty with any particular questions? If a student finds an error or problem, point it out to the rest of the class.

At the end of the test collect all papers and answer sheets and count each for accuracy.

Try to mark these papers quickly. Your students will be anxious for the results. Give the tests back to the students and go over each question. Have the students place the tests in their folders. If you have a policy that all test papers must have a parent's signature, be sure to follow up and see that the tests were signed.

Try not to embarrass any child for failing a test. Some teachers call the student's name and grade aloud. This can be humiliating to a child. If you'd like to call them up to your desk, that is fine; there you can talk to them privately.

There are other ways to evaluate students: teacher-student conferences, oral reports, student work, journal writing or student portfolios. For a more objective view of your students you may want to consider using these in addition to testing.

Student Portfolios

Student portfolios have been used for many years, and now there is serious talk about making them count in grading or as an alternative to standardized testing.

What is a student portfolio? A portfolio is a collection of student work to reflect his/her progress and best work. Portfolios allow students to demonstrate growth and change. They also allow students to learn to self-assess.

If your school decides to use student portfolios here are a few guidelines:

1. Decide what will be in the portfolio. Will it include just samples of students' work or will transcripts, and test scores also be allowed?
2. Guide students on what to include in their portfolios.
3. Clean out portfolios regularly (once a month) so the students will be forced to decide what work really represents their best work.
4. If the portfolios are used for grading, ensure that they are evaluated fairly.

    a. Make sure the criteria for scoring is public.
    b. Create models of what a good portfolio looks like.
    c. Ensure that there is more than one single reader/evaluator.
    d. Establish an appeals process.[11]

Testing is a tool. It is a means to an end. Test scores are helpful and important, but they do not measure all abilities and talents. What they do is give us a great deal of information that can be used to help us understand each student better. By understanding each student's strengths and weaknesses we can then provide each student with the best possible education.

ENDNOTES

1. National School Public Relations Association Standardized Aptitude and Achievement Testing, Arlington, NYSUT, pp. 4–5. 1978.
2. Ibid. pp. 7–8.
3. Sparzo, Frank J.: Preparing Better Teacher Made Tests: A Practical Guide. *Phi Delta Kappa,* pp. 19–21. 1990.
4. Ibid. pp. 19–21.
5. Ibid. pp. 22–25.
6. Noll, Victor H. and Scannell, Dale P.: *Introduction to Educational Measurement.* Boston, Houghton, pp. 221–231. 1972.
7. Sparzo, op. cit., pp. 26–27.
8. Ibid. pp. 29–30.
9. Noll, op. cit., pp. 202–204.
10. Ibid. pp. 205–206.
11. Wolf, Dennie Palmer and Mitchell, Ruth: Student Portfolios: Good-bye to Multiple Choice? *American Teacher,* V 76, p. 2. May/June 1992.

Chapter Fourteen

FIRST ENCOUNTERS

Frequent Problems of First-Year Teachers

"**I** can't teach. I have discipline problems. I can't get any supplies. Where are the textbooks? I can't teach without books. There's too much paper work."

There's no doubt, your first year of teaching will be the most challenging. There are many adjustments to be made and there will be some problems. It doesn't matter if you teach in a small rural classroom or an inner city school, the problems are the same. It may help you to review these common problems and take heart in the fact that you are not alone.

Supplies and Materials

Many teachers are upset when supplies and materials are not ready and waiting for them. In most schools you must requisition supplies and materials. I had to borrow chalk and an eraser for the first few days of school and I had to wait several weeks for textbooks. It is very frustrating trying to teach without the proper materials. Should you go out and buy your own supplies? Only the necessities and only if you can't borrow them. One new teacher went out and spent two hundred dollars on her credit card for supplies. Not only did she find out that the school would not reimburse her, but her students found these things neat and pocketed them. Find out the school policy and procedures for ordering supplies and materials. Be patient, then nag! Remember, "the squeaky wheel gets the most oil."

Scheduling

Each teacher must create a schedule for teaching, Monday–Friday from nine o'clock to three o'clock. You must decide when to teach reading, math, English, science, social studies, physical education, music, art, health science and computer lab. Once you have your schedule together, there will be a knock at the door. It may be the Librarian, TAG Teacher, Speech Teacher, Resource Room Teacher or Physical Education Teacher trying to schedule a convenient time to meet with your class or pull some students out of class for special services. How should you handle this scheduling mess? Be flexible, be kind, and be strong. It is a nightmare to see your schedule ripped apart. Keep in mind that these teachers provide necessary services for your students. Together you are a team. It takes a great deal of time and patience to work out a new and revised schedule, but the results are worth it. Hang in there, by next year you will be a "pro" at scheduling and rescheduling!

Workload

When you embark on a teaching career, you are in no way prepared for the paper work. All you've dreamt about is teaching your own class. Planning, preparing and presenting your lessons keep you busy. Then there are: attendance records, lunch forms, emergency cards, health cards, anecdotal records and roll books just to mention a few. How do you handle the workload? Stay calm and stay on top of the paper work. Do not put it off, do it as soon as you can because there may be more forms or reports tomorrow. If you do get swamped, ask for help or extra time. Most supervisors understand and will extend the deadline. Don't abuse the extension, get the work done and try not to ask for extensions too often. I used my lunch hour and my preparation periods to do most of the paper work. It meant grading papers and writing my plans at home, but at least I was able to keep abreast of the paper work.

Disciplinary Problems

Every class has at least one disciplinary problem. It is unnerving and frustrating for any teacher to have a disruptive student. Instead of teaching you spend your day disciplining the student or students. Valuable teaching and learning time is lost. What should you do? First, find your copy of the school disciplinary code. Read this to refresh your memory about the disciplinary procedures in your school—when to keep a record of the outbursts, sending students to the office, and suspension procedures will be outlined in this booklet. Second, check with the previous teacher to find out what actions work best with this child.

Third, be sure you are using good classroom management techniques, or it could be said that you have no control in the classroom. Fourth, let the students know YOU are in charge. Be consistent and be fair. You are there to teach, not police!

Overload

New teachers have a tendency to go overboard during their first year. They put all their time and energy into developing creative and motivating lessons. One new teacher would get dressed in costume to teach history. She also used charts, graphs, the overhead projector, puppets and music in her lesson. The children were entertained, but failed to understand the material she was presenting.

Other teachers try to take on too much their first year. They sign up for every course, volunteer for lunch duty, after school center and bus duty. They spread themselves too thin. What should you do?

Take it easy your first year. Concentrate on your teaching. Develop one creative and motivating lesson each week. Try new ideas. Do not take on added responsibility unless you are ready. Take one course or workshop that you feel will help you most. Take the time to evaluate your teaching and make changes where necessary. Relax and enjoy your new career.

Safety

Today many teachers, new and old, worry about their safety on the job. What can you do to ensure your safety? Find out about the school and neighborhood around your school. Ask the office where it is safe to park. Do not arrive too early, nor be the last one to leave the school building. If you are alone in your classroom, keep the door locked. Keep your valuables in a locked closet or drawer. If you should leave the building late at night, parent-teacher conference, leave with other teachers. These are just some basic safety tips; practice them for safety first.

Isolation

Isolation is often a problem for new teachers. No one really has time to help them because they are busy with their own classrooms, especially during the first few weeks of school. Even the supervisor who says "Come to me with any questions," very often has little time to give. What should you do? Talk to the school secretary. Very often she can suggest someone who can help you. She knows the teachers and which ones will have time to give you assistance. You can also frequent the Faculty Room and ask lots of questions. You'll get lots of answers and may make some friendships to combat your feeling of isolation.

Advice and Independence

New teachers are confused when fellow teachers offer advice. After all you are just out of school and you know the latest techniques. You want to be independent and do it your way, yet the other teachers are experienced and probably know best. All of a sudden your confidence wanes and you are filled with self-doubt. How should you handle advice? Listen, always listen to your colleagues, they often have some valuable insights. For example, they may share their thoughts on disciplinary actions that worked with a particular child last year. Or they may know that the Supervisor puts great emphasis on the reading program. This advice can be useful. On the other hand, some advice may not be useful. For example, the only way to teach vocabulary is through drill, drill, drill. Or children should be tested weekly in all academic areas or they won't learn.

Be polite, listen and then use the advice you feel is useful and discard the advice you cannot use. Do not be intimidated, or worry about hurting anyone's feelings. You can always say you tried it, but it didn't work and thank them for their help. You'll find the balance you need to feel independent in no time.

Being Observed

This is a real concern of new teachers. That very first observation is unnerving. You don't know what to expect or what is expected of you. Remember that everyone survives an observation. All teachers, new and old, go through the same process, with the same butterflies and weak knees. What should you do? Stay calm. Prepare your lessons carefully. Smile and do your best.

These are some primary concerns of new teachers. I'm sure that you will be able to add to this list after your first few months as a new teacher.

One last thought I'd like to share is not to let any problem get to you or cause you to give up teaching. Problems can be solved if you really try. It may mean leaving that school or situation and finding a different teaching situation. Many teachers leave and throw their careers away for one bad situation. There are many ways to teach and to be a teacher and it is not always inside a classroom.

Keep yourself healthy. Eat right, take vitamins, exercise and get plenty of sleep. When you're feeling great, problems do not seem so bad. You can think clearly and you can do a better job.

Accept each new challenge as a chance to learn and grow. You'll be surprised how your confidence will grow too!

Chapter Fifteen

LAW REVIEW—TEACHERS AND THE LAW

How Much Do You Know About School Law?
Can You Answer This Question:
Corporal Punishment is Not Unconstitutional
True   Or   False

The answer is true, corporal punishment is not unconstitutional. Yet, the use of corporal punishment as a disciplinary measure in the public schools remains a controversial issue. The question being: Do teachers have the right to inflict pain and humiliation on students? Some states prohibit corporal punishment, but in other states it is the local ordinance that may prohibit its use. You must be aware of your school district's policies on corporal punishment. Parents can and do file suit against teachers and school districts if the punishment has been excessive. School officials must be able to demonstrate in court that all other remedies short of corporal punishment were tried unsuccessfully prior to administration of the corporal punishment.[1]

Here are some other law issues you should be aware of:

Due Process

Children, students in particular, have not always been given the privilege of due process. Many have been expelled without adequate hearing or have been required to accept severe and unfair treatment. Two important court cases have provided new guidelines.[2]

Before a student faces suspension or expulsion:

1. Prior notification must be given that this penalty will be imposed.
2. The specific reason for imposing this penalty must be stated.
3. An opportunity for a hearing regarding the charges must be offered.
4. A fair decision must be rendered.

141

Equal Protection

The equal protection clause protects the handicapped, and other identifiable groups such as Blacks, Hispanics, or females, and guarantees none of these are singled out for different treatment than received by other students.[3]

Freedom of Speech and the Press

School authorities are not permitted to deny a student his fundamental right (freedom of speech) simply because of a "mere desire to avoid discomfort and unpleasantness that always accompany an unpopular viewpoint."[4]

As far as freedom of the press is concerned, students can be disciplined for conduct or for actions associated with publishing and distributing materials. Students have a legal responsibility to avoid activities that provide substantial or material disruption of the educational environment or which infringe on the rights of others.[5]

Search and Seizure

Teachers and other school officials may conduct searches and seizures on their own authority without a warrant if there's probable cause. Teachers should strictly follow the pertinent rules and procedures developed by the school district.[6]

Student Marriage and Pregnancy

Students cannot be denied an education or restricted from participation in the full range of school activities including graduation exercises because of pregnancy or marriage.[7]

Religious Expression

Separation of Church and State continues to cause controversy both in and out of the public school system. Courts have declared school prayer, Bible reading and the use of public school facilities for religious instruction to be unconstitutional. To date the issue of school prayer is still being challenged in the Supreme Court.[8]

Grading Practices

Punishment should not affect a student's grades, credits or graduation unless the punishment is for specific academic dishonesty. Reducing grades as a form of punishment has been challenged in the courts. Base your decisions solely on academic performance.

A diploma cannot be denied as a result of disciplinary infraction.[9]

In addition to knowing your students' rights, teachers need to be aware that they can be held liable for any and all negligent behavior.

This entire chapter is not meant to intimidate you, but rather to inform you about some important legal issues in education — issues that directly affect you and your job. Teachers need to be kept informed about these legal issues from day one. I was in graduate school before I learned the legal aspects of my job.

The items that follow are important for you to note and remember. Read them carefully and keep them handy for reference during the school year.

1. A class may not be left unattended or unsupervised during the course of the school day. Any emergency should be handled by contacting the school office, supervisor or the teacher next door.
2. Children who leave your room for any reason (to go on a message, bathroom or office) are still your responsibility. Before they leave be sure they know the behavior expected of them.
3. Physical punishment of children must be avoided at all times. Physical force may be used only to the extent absolutely essential for restraint in the face of danger.
4. Children may not be used to render personal service for a teacher. They cannot be sent to the store or Faculty Room to get you a cup of coffee.
5. No child should be sent home without authorization. A parent or legal guardian must sign out a child after receiving office approval.
6. No child should be kept more than ten minutes after school without prior parent notification.
7. Personal property of pupils may not be destroyed or thrown away. Provide an opportunity for the parent or guardian to retrieve the item.
8. No drug or medicine should be administered by a teacher.
9. No child is to be denied lunch, especially as a disciplinary action.
10. Money may not be collected from children without authorization from the supervisor.
11. No student may be permitted to go on a field trip without a signed parental permission slip.

12. Gym and Laboratory classes present a high safety risk. Teachers must supervise properly to prevent accidental injury. Failure to provide necessary safety instructions and safety equipment can result in liability. Poorly maintained equipment can also cause injury. Be sure to check all equipment before using it with your students.

13. Personal information regarding a child (address, telephone number, parents' name) is not to be given to any person other than authorized staff.

14. Official pupil records and documents should never be taken out of the school.

15. No class is to be dismissed before dismissal time unless authorized by the supervisor.

16. Pupil or student injury must be reported to the office immediately, as well as fire.

17. Suspected cases of child abuse must be discretely reported to the Supervisor.

18. All visitors to your classroom must show a visitors pass from the office.

19. Teachers may not leave the school building during preparation periods without proper approval and must sign out and sign in upon returning.

20. Money which has been collected should not be left in school since most school districts do not take responsibility unless the money is placed in the school safe.

21. No instructional or audio/visual equipment may be removed or borrowed without written permission.

22. The school is not responsible for personal articles left unattended. This includes your wallet. I can't tell you how many times I lost my wallet in a locked closet. Always take it with you!

23. Windows without screens may not be opened more than eight inches from the bottom.

24. Unsafe conditions (peeling paint, broken desks, broken windows) must be reported in writing to the office and get a dated received receipt.

25. Teachers are responsible to keep abreast of legal issues and the ramifications of current court decisions on their own actions in the classroom. [11,12]

The influence of the courts on the conduct of teachers and administrators is a great one. Issues will continue to arise and be challenged by the courts. It is the Superintendent's responsibility to make sure all teachers are aware of the legal aspects of teaching. Please check with your Superintendent for a copy of the School District regulations. Whenever in doubt about a regulation ask your supervisor and see if you can get it in writing to be extra safe. It may keep you and your school out of court!

ENDNOTES

1. Nolte, M.C.: "Before You Can Take a Paddling to Court, Read This Corporal Punishment Advice." *American School Board Journal,* V.35 pp. 173–227, 1987.
2. Goss v Lopez 419 US 565, 42 (1975). Gault 387 US 1 (1967).
3. Martin, R.: *Legal Issues in Behavior Modification.* Champaign, Research Press, 1975.
4. Tinker v Des Moines Independent School District 393 US 503, 89 S Ct. 733 (1969).
5. Bartlett, L.: *Student Press and Distribution Issues: Rights and Responsibilities.* Reston, NASSP 1987.
6. People v Jackson 65 Misc. 2d 909, 319 NYS 2d. 731 (1971).
7. Board of Education Harrodsburg vs Bentley 383 S.W. 2d. 677 (1964).
8. Engel v Vitale 370 US 421, 82 S CT. 1261 (1962). School District of Abington Township v Shempp and Murray and Curlett 374 US 203, 83 S CT. 1560 (1963).
9. Bartlett L.: "Don't Mix: A Critical Review." *Journal of Law and Education,* V 16 pp. 155–165 (1987).
10. Morrissey, Virginia: "Law Refresher." Board of Education of New York City, Community School District 24, Queens. 1980.
11. Alexander, Kern: *School Law.* St. Paul, West, 1980.
12. Morrissey, op. cit., p. 3.

Chapter Sixteen

FIRST AID

Goals:

1. Preserve life.
2. Prevent the injury or conditions from becoming worse.
3. Promote recovery.
   (American Medical Association, 1988)

Do you know what to do if one of your students: faints, chokes, vomits or gets a nosebleed?

Most accidental injuries are minor and easily treated with simple first aid techniques. A quick response can make all the difference. The more knowledge you have immediately at hand, the more useful you can be in an emergency. Your school should have a first aid kit and guide. Find out where it is located. You will also need to ask about school policy. When an accident occurs, what steps should you take? Who do you notify first (office, principal or nurse)?

On the following pages you will find basic first aid instructions. This is not a substitute for the practical experience you can gain if you attend first aid classes, but by familiarizing yourself with these techniques you will be able to act swiftly and efficiently in any emergency.

Before administering first aid you must:

1. Summon HELP.
2. Find out what happened without endangering yourself.
3. Reassure and protect the person from any further danger.
4. Deal with the injury or condition as required and to arrange travel to a hospital if necessary.[1]

Bleeding

To stop a nosebleed: Apply direct pressure to both nostrils by firmly pinching with thumb and forefinger. The student should sit down and lean slightly forward. Keep pinching until bleeding stops, about ten minutes. Seek medical help if bleeding continues for longer than twenty minutes, or if you suspect the nose may be broken.

Minor Cuts and Scrapes

Pressing a clean gauze pad over the wound for a few minutes helps to stop the bleeding. When bleeding has stopped, clean around the cut with a clean gauze or antiseptic pad by wiping from the edges outward. Small cuts heal rapidly when left uncovered, but students may request a band aid.

Severe Bleeding

Your main aim is to reduce blood flow to encourage the clotting of blood in the wound to seal the damaged blood vessels. This can be done by applying pressure to the wound itself. As a general rule, keep the injured part raised above the level of the heart. After you have administered first aid, seek emergency medical help.

Broken Bones

If there is any bleeding from the wound, treat that first. Do not try to manipulate bone back into position. While waiting for help keep the child warm and comfortable. Give nothing to eat or drink. Get assistance and move the child as little as possible. If you must move the child, immobilize the limb in the most comfortable position by using splints. If ambulance is not necessary, take child to the emergency room.

Splints

A splint is a support used to immobilize an injured part of the body (usually an arm or leg) to reduce pain and further injury. Always secure in two places, but not too close to the injury. In an emergency a broom handle, rolled up newspaper or a pillow taped around an injured arm can make an effective splint. Use wide lengths of material or bandages and do not tie too tightly.

Burns and Scalds

If a student should get burnt or scalded, immerse the burned area immediately in tap or cool water or apply clean, cool, moist towels. Do not use ice.

Choking

Choking occurs when food or a foreign object obstructs the throat and interferes with normal breathing. Follow these steps if a choking student is unable to speak or cough forcefully.

1. Stand behind the student or his chair if the student is seated.
2. Wrap your arms around the student's waist.
3. Place your fist with the thumb side between the student's naval and rib cage.
4. Place your other hand over the fist and make a quick upward thrust, exerting pressure into the student's abdomen.
5. Repeat if necessary. If the obstruction cannot be removed, call for medical help promptly.

Convulsive Seizures

Convulsive seizures are often associated with epilepsy, although they can also be caused by high fever, head injuries and electrical shock.

Convulsive seizures can last two to five minutes, after which normal breathing resumes. If you see a student having a convulsive seizure, you can help:

1. Protect him from nearby hazards.
2. Loosen his shirt collar.
3. Place a folded jacket under his head.
4. Turn him on his side to keep the airway clear.
5. If a seizure lasts for more than ten minutes, then take the student to the emergency room for an evaluation.

Eye Trauma

A student may get something caught in an eye. If a student gets a speck of dirt on the outside of the eyeball or inside of the eyelid: Keep the student from rubbing the eye. Have the student blink and try to make tears. Wash your hand thoroughly before examining the student's eye. Pull down the lower lid to see if the speck is on the inner surface of the lid. If so, gently lift it with the corner of a clean handkerchief. If it is on the inside of the upper lid have the student look down and grasp the lashes of the upper lid gently between the thumb and forefinger and pull the lid out and down over the lower lid. This may dislodge the dirt.

Flush the eye with clean water, use an eyedropper or small bulb syringe. If these steps do not work, put a clean bandage over both eyes gently and get medical help. Covering both eyes is preferable because movement of the eye that is not injured will cause damage to the eye that is damaged. Young children may be frightened if you cover both eyes so try to reassure them.

If a student gets a chemical or other hazardous substance in his eyes, rinse immediately with water. Flush the eye for at least three to five minutes. Then go to the doctor or emergency room.

Fainting

Fainting results from inadequate blood supply to the brain. If a student feels faint: Have him bend his head down between his knees. Or if possible have him lie down with his head lower than his feet. If a child has fainted: Keep him lying down as above and loosen his clothing. After he recovers, a drink of juice might help. If he does not recover in a short while, seek medical help.

Insect Bites and Stings

First aid for mild insect bites (such as bee stings) is not always successful because part of the bite is under the skin. There are a few things that you can do: If a bee leaves a stinger, scrape it off gently, working from the side. Do not squeeze the stinger. Applying a paste of baking soda or a pad soaked with plenty of water and a little ammonia may make the bite feel better. A cold wet cloth helps too! Calamine lotion helps to stop the itch.

Poisoning
1-800-942-5969 National Poison Control Center

In case of poisoning, call a doctor, poison control center, hospital or emergency rescue unit promptly. Explain what unusual symptoms the student is showing, what substance may have been involved (trade name, manufacturer, label warning) and the student's name, age, weight and general health.

Rescue Breathing

If a student stops breathing, it's important that you react immediately. Here is a list of things to do:

1. Check for unresponsiveness. Shake student gently and shout "Are you Okay?"
2. Shout HELP! Have someone get help.
3. Position the student on his back. Roll him toward you by pulling evenly from his hip and shoulder.
4. Open the airway. Tilt the head back and lift the chin with fingers under the body part of the jaw.
5. Check for breathlessness. Look, listen and feel for breathing for three to five seconds.
6. Give two full breaths. With head tilted back, pinch the nose. Seal your lips around the victims mouth. Give 2 full breaths for 1 to 1½ seconds each.
7. Check for a pulse at the side of the neck.
8. Phone emergency medical services for help.
9. Begin rescue breathing. Keep head tilted back. Pinch the nose. Seal your lips and give 1 breath every 5 seconds. Look, listen and feel for breathing between breaths.
10. Recheck pulse every minute for 5–10 seconds. If the student has a pulse, but is not breathing continue rescue breathing.

* Remember this information should not take the place of CPR Training. Call your local Red Cross for information on these courses.

Shock

Shock usually accompanies severe injury or emotional upset. In any first aid emergency, always keep in mind that the student may be in shock. Signs of shock include: cold, clammy skin, a pale face, chills, confusion, frequent nausea or vomiting and shallow breathing. While waiting for emergency help you should:

1. Have the student lie down with the legs elevated.
2. Keep the student covered to prevent loss of body heat.
3. Give the student fluids if he is able to swallow, unless abdominal injury is suspected.

Tooth Loss or Injury

Trauma to the teeth usually results from a fall. Pick up the tooth or teeth that are knocked out and gently rinse them off without handling the root. Wrap them in a clean gauze and dampen it. The roots must be kept moist if there is a chance to save the tooth. Clean the broken teeth and blood from the victim's mouth. Use a sterile gauze pad and have the victim put it over the socket where the tooth is missing and bite down firmly on the gauze. Take the victim and the teeth to the dentist promptly.

Vomiting

In children, vomiting can be caused by almost any physical or emotional upset, but it is most likely to be caused by an infection of the digestive tract.

A child may be frightened and upset, they need you to be calm and sympathetic. When the vomiting stops, give the child some water to rinse out their mouth and sponge his/her face. Encourage the child to lie down and rest. There is a danger of dehydration, encourage the child to periodically sip some liquids to guard against dehydration.

Recognizing Common Health Problems

Teachers can often spot potential health problems and alert the parents before they become serious. Here are a few to look for:

Head lice

Head lice are insects that rely on humans for food, warmth and moisture. They spend their entire life on a person's head. The most common sign of head lice is itching. A student who is scratching his head constantly may have head lice.

Impetigo

Impetigo is a skin infection caused by several types of bacteria. The following are symptoms of impetigo: A small blister filled with a watery fluid or a boil that contains pus-like material. A "green crust," which appears several days later when the blister or boil breaks open. Children with impetigo should stay at home until they are seen by a doctor and they are free from infection.

Scabies

Scabies is a skin disease caused by an almost invisible organism, the "itch mite." Because of its highly contagious nature, scabies often spreads among school age children quite rapidly. The only way to find out whether or not a person has scabies is to see a doctor. But these symptoms are quite common: a red, itchy rash, linear burrows appearing between the fingers, on the elbows, hands, wrists or other susceptible areas, and intense itching, especially at night.

Conjunctivitis

Conjunctivitis is best known as "pink eye." It is a sticky discharge caused by the inflammation of the membrane covering the eye and lining the eyelids. The symptoms are very "blood shot" eyes. It is very contagious and the child must be sent home immediately. A doctor will prescribe drops and when the treatment is complete the child may return to school.

Visual and Hearing Problems

If a student exhibits any of the following symptoms or behavior, he may have a visual problem:

rubbing eyes	continual blinking
squinting	holding a book at a distance
reading for brief periods	reading with his nose in a book
headaches	frequent accidents
general inattention	craning neck to see better

If a student has a hearing problem, he may exhibit some of these symptoms:

reading lips

turning head to hear you better

positioning himself with his peers to hear them better

inability to follow simple verbal directions

If you should identify any medical problems you should alert the parents. You may want to document your findings, your conversation with the parent and outcome. Follow up to ensure the child has been seen by a physician. If the child has not been seen by the doctor, you may want to discuss this with your supervisor for further action.

Accident Report

An accident report is a written record of how the accident happened. Some schools have forms which you fill out with such details as: date, time, what happened, where it happened, who was involved, what actions were taken, and the names of several witnesses. In other schools, you must supply a written explanation including the above mentioned particulars. Each witness must also write a note explaining what they saw. Check with your school office for the appropriate forms. Ask too for the First Aid Kit, Guide, and procedures for emergencies.

Some Concluding Thoughts

Due to the rapid spread of AIDS, school districts are providing classroom teachers with plastic gloves and antiseptic gauze pads to be kept in your desk. Should a student begin to bleed, it is in your own best interest to use your gloves. School districts are also providing inservice training in first aid techniques. Part of this training includes discussion about the transmission of AIDS and how to protect yourself.

ENDNOTES

American Medical Association: *Home Medical Advisor.* New York, Random House, 1988.

American Red Cross: *Standard First Aid and Personal Safety.* Garden City, Doubleday, 1979.

Paraprofessional and School Related Personnel: *Safe and Healthy Schools: The Employees Guide to Student First Aid and Health Problems.* Washington, D.C., AFT, 1984.

Chapter Seventeen

WHAT YOU SHOULD KNOW ABOUT AIDS

Take This Mini Quiz to See How Much You Know About AIDS.

Answer True or False

1. People can look and feel healthy and still transmit the AIDS virus.
2. There is a vaccine to prevent AIDS.
3. Women cannot transmit the AIDS virus.
4. AIDS can be transmitted by sitting next to someone in class who has the AIDS virus.
5. A person can get AIDS from giving blood.
6. Everyone infected with the AIDS virus has developed AIDS.
7. AIDS, itself, usually does not kill a person.
8. Most children with AIDS got it from an infected mother.

(Answer key: 1. True, 2. False, 3. False, 4. False, 5. False, 6. False, 7. True, 8. True.)[1]

You have no doubt received some AIDS education at the university level and you will receive further information and training from the district which employs you. Many teachers are concerned about contracting AIDS from their students; others are uneasy about the disease and how it is transmitted. If you have similar concerns, you are not alone. This chapter was designed to address these concerns.

What Is AIDS?

AIDS stands for acquired immunodeficiency syndrome. It is an infectious disease caused by a virus that can damage the brain and destroy the body's ability to fight off illness. AIDS by itself doesn't kill. But it allows other infections to invade the body, and these diseases can kill (such as pneumonia, cancer and other illnesses).

At the present time there is no known cure for AIDS, and no vaccine that prevents the disease.

Fortunately the AIDS virus is hard to catch and can be prevented. AIDS is a very serious disease, but you should know these facts:

1. AIDS is not spread by casual contact in school, at parties, in swimming pools, stores or on the job site.

2. You can't catch AIDS by hugging, shaking hands or simply being near a person who is infected with the virus. No person has ever been infected by an insect bite.

3. You can't catch AIDS from a toilet seat.

How Do People Get AIDS?

Not everyone is at risk for AIDS. People who are at risk can protect themselves if they take reasonable precautions. It starts with knowing how people get AIDS.

There are three main ways the AIDS virus is spread:

1. Having sex with an infected person.
2. Sharing drug needles and syringes with users of heroin, cocaine and other illegal drugs.
3. Babies can be born with the virus if the mother has been infected.

What About Blood Transfusions?

It is true that some people got AIDS from infected blood transfusions. But that's extremely rare. Today all donated blood is tested for the AIDS virus. There is also no risk from donating blood. New equipment is used for each donor, each time blood is given.

How Can you Tell If You Have The AIDS Virus?

The only way to tell if you have the AIDS virus is by having a blood test. The test looks for changes in your blood caused by the presence of the virus. If you test positive, it means that you have been infected.

You can have the virus without having the disease itself, or without even appearing or feeling ill. And you can transmit the virus to others.

Once infected you will remain infected for life. It could take years for the disease to develop, or it may never develop. Others developed AIDS Related Complex (ARC), which symptoms may include: fatigue, weight loss, diarrhea, fever chills, night sweats, and swollen glands. These symptoms last longer than they would in other illnesses, such as the flu. Some people with ARC may never develop AIDS.

How To Protect Yourself

The safest way to avoid being infected by the AIDS virus is to avoid promiscuous sex and illegal drugs. You can get AIDS from one sexual experience. Your risk of becoming infected increases dramatically if you have more than one sexual partner. If you or your partner have more than one sexual partner, you should reduce your risk by using condoms.

AIDS Education

Education about AIDS begins in early elementary school and in some instances at home. It is very important that children grow up knowing which behaviors to avoid to protect themselves from exposure to the AIDS virus. You, as the teacher, will be providing this education both formally in your classroom and informally when students come to you with questions. Teachers need to be well informed about AIDS and your school district will provide this service.

You will receive general training about:

1. The nature of the AIDS epidemic and means of controlling its spread.
2. The role of the school in providing education to prevent the transmission of HIV.
3. Methods and materials to accomplish effective programs of school health education about AIDS.
4. School policies for students and staff who may be infected.[2]

In addition, you will receive more specific training about providing effective health education about AIDS through inservice training programs. In other words, you will be adequately prepared to teach your students about the AIDS virus.

Your next concern may be: What exactly will I be teaching? The principle purpose of education about AIDS is to prevent HIV infection. The program should assure that young people acquire the knowledge and skills they need to adopt and maintain types of behavior that virtually eliminate their risk of becoming infected.

In the early elementary grades, the program is designed to allay excessive fears of the epidemic and of becoming infected. The basic concepts that are taught are:

AIDS is a disease that is causing some adults to get very sick, but it does not commonly affect children.

AIDS is very hard to get. You cannot get it just by being near or touching someone who has it.

Scientists all over the world are working hard to find a way to stop people from getting AIDS and to cure those who have it.

In the late elementary and middle grades the program provides the following information:

Viruses can be transmitted from an infected person to an uninfected person through various means.

Some viruses cause disease among people.

Persons who are infected with some viruses that cause disease may not have any signs or symptoms of disease.

AIDS is caused by a virus that weakens the ability of infected individuals to fight off disease.

People who are infected with the AIDS virus live in every state in the United States and in most other countries of the world. People of all races, nationalities and religions are infected. Males and females alike.

The AIDS virus can be transmitted by sexual contact with an infected person, by using needles and other injection equipment that an infected person has used, and from an infected mother to her infant before or during birth.

It sometimes takes several years after becoming infected with the AIDS virus before symptoms of the disease appear.

Most infected people who developed symptoms of AIDS only lived for about two years after their symptoms were diagnosed. Now thanks to experimental drugs their life span has been increased.

The AIDS virus cannot be caught by touching someone who is infected, by being in the same room with an infected person, or by donating blood.[3]

In the junior and senior high school grades the curriculum is quite specific, using such terms as: rectum, vagina, penis, intercourse, french kissing and condom. This education is usually provided by the school health education teacher as part of the health education curriculum. In the elementary grades the regular classroom teacher provides the education.

Can I Get AIDS From a Student Who Has AIDS?

Casual social contact between children and persons infected with the AIDS virus is not dangerous.

None of the identified cases of AIDS in the United States are known or are suspected to have been transmitted from one child to another in school, day care, or foster care settings. Transmission would necessitate exposure of open cuts to the blood or other body fluids of the infected child, a highly unlikely occurrence. Even then routine safety procedures for handling blood or other body fluids would be effective in preventing transmission from children with AIDS to other children in the school.[4] As an extra precaution many schools are providing plastic gloves and antiseptic pads and band aids to be used by the teacher whenever a child is bleeding.

AIDS is a life threatening disease and a major public health issue. Its impact on our society is and will continue to be devastating. However, AIDS is preventable. It is the responsibility of everyone to be informed about AIDS and to exercise the appropriate preventive measures. The lives of our young people depend on us.[5]

Additional Informational Sources

U.S. Public Health Service
Public Affairs Office
Hubert H. Humphrey Blvd.
Room 725 H
200 Independence Avenue SW
Washington, D.C. 20201
(202) 245 6867

American Red Cross
AIDS Education Office
1730 D Street NW
Washington, D.C. 20006
(202) 737 8300

HOTLINES

PHS AIDS HOTLINE
(800) 342 2437

NATIONAL SEXUALLY TRANSMITTED DISEASE HOTLINE
(800) 227 8922

NATIONAL GAY TASK FORCE
(800) 221 7044

ENDNOTES

1. MASSAPEQUA PUBLIC SCHOOLS: *Curriculum Guide on AIDS*. Massapequa, Nassau County, New York, pp. 1–2 1988.
2. Center for Disease Control: *Guidelines for Effective School Health Education to Prevent the Spread of AIDS*. Washington, D.C., Morbidity and Mortality Weekly Report, p. 3 Jan. 1988.
3. Ibid. p. 4–6.
4. Koop, Everett C.: Surgeon General's Report on AIDS Washington, D.C., U.S. Department of Health and Human Services p. 4 1986.
5. Ibid. p. 8.

Chapter Eighteen

CHILD ABUSE AND NEGLECT: WHAT YOU NEED TO KNOW

About 1,300 children nationwide were reported to have died from abuse or neglect in 1986, according to the National Committee for Prevention of Child Abuse. More than 100 of those deaths were in New York City. Authorities say most of the deaths are a result of negligence rather than brutality by parents or guardians. Only a handful of abuse cases result in criminal charges for murder or manslaughter.

In every state, educators are required by law to report suspected child abuse. This includes teachers, principals, counselors, school nurses and staff members in day care centers and summer camps.

Educators do not have to know that abuse actually took place. By law, a suspicion of child abuse generally means that the person who does the reporting has "reasonable cause to believe" or "reasonable cause to know or suspect" that the child has been mistreated.

There are a wide range of indicators that could signal the presence of neglect or of physical, emotional or sexual abuse in children. These may include:

• Extensive bruises, especially around the head or face, fractures, lacerations, whiplike marks, awkward movements or soreness, extreme sensitivity to pain.

• Withdrawal of interest in school, poorer than normal performance, behavioral problems, wariness of adult contact, apprehensiveness when other children cry, fear of parents or going home, unexplained absences.

• Psychosomatic illnesses, delays in speaking and understanding language, immature behavior for age group.

• In the case of sexual abuse, seemingly promiscuous behavior or more sexual knowledge than appropriate for the child's age, pregnancy, VD, difficulty in walking or sitting, torn stained or bloody under clothing, pain or itching in the genital area, unwillingness to change for gym, withdrawn infantile behavior, poor peer relationships or delinquency.

• In cases of neglect, abandonment, unattended physical or medical needs, hunger, poor hygiene or inappropriate clothing for the weather, begging or stealing food, constant fatigue, listlessness or falling asleep in class, alcohol or drug abuse or extended stays at school.

• In some states the laws go further to include circumstances that could result in future child abuse, for example, if a teacher learned that a child would be unsupervised while parents were vacationing.

Educators should keep notes on the child's appearance, bruises or actions that have given them reason to suspect abuse as well as on any contacts with the parents or other school officials.

How Do You Report Child Abuse?

In most states, reports may be made orally to the appropriate agency, usually the social services, family services or child-protective services department. In many school districts, the law allows teachers to report to the principal, who is responsible for notifying authorities. Some communities have hot lines for telephone reports.

Many states require that the oral report be followed by a written report, usually within 24–48 hours. School district policy may require that school officials receive a copy of the report, which is kept in a confidential file separate from the child's school records.

Educators should contact their district office for specific regulations in their area.

After a report is made the social-service agency will begin an investigation, talk to the teacher and other school personnel, interview the family to substantiate or negate the suspicions.

During the investigation, it is important for school staff members to be supportive of the parents as well as the child, recognizing that the family as a whole may need to receive professional help. A hostile approach may cause the family to withdraw further.

Teachers and administrators should make themselves available to the child and parents, to listen to their concerns. The teacher may want to schedule a conference with the parents even before the reporting.

It is natural for a teacher to become involved, because he or she sees the child daily and is aware of the child's behavior and appearance. But the teacher should avoid playing the role of investigator or therapist.

School personnel need to be aware of their district's policies on dealing with allegations of abuse before the situation arises.

It is also a good idea to discuss with an administrator what support the teacher will receive after making the report, if the parents become hostile or try to remove the child from class.

You can be held liable if you do not report suspicions that a child has been abused.

State laws generally provide that failure to report is a crime, usually a misdemeanor. Penalties vary by state, but may range from a few days in jail to a year's imprisonment and a $1,000 fine. Criminal liability occurs only if the educator willfully or knowingly fails to report. However, educators may be judged to have civil liability for negligence of their duties and be subject to legal and administrative penalties.

Notifying a superior—rather than the appropriate agency—does not release a teacher from liability until a report is made. Some administrators may not be aware of their legal responsibility, or may think that reporting will reflect negatively on their school. It is also important to remember that failure to report may leave the child in serious danger.

Most cases of child abuse do not get to court. In those few cases that do, however, it is likely that the child's teacher would be called to testify to the child's behavior or appearance on specific occasions.

If your suspicions turn out to be unfounded, can a parent sue the school officials? It is highly unlikely that an educator would be sued for reporting, and, if this did happen, the educator who reported in good faith would not be found liable. All states provide immunity or protection from liability for a professional who reports suspected child abuse.

Where Can You Get More Information?

The National Child Abuse Hot Line can refer callers to authorities in their area. This service can also provide educators with advice on specific cases or how to report abuse. Children can also call this toll-free number to receive advice. The number is in operation 24 hours a day (800) 422-4453.

The National Education Association's 1987 handbook for teachers, *How Schools Can Help Combat Child Abuse and Neglect,* is available from the N.E.A. Professional Library, P.O. Box 509, West Haven, Connecticut 06516.

The National Committee for Prevention of Child Abuse publishes a catalog, listing many pamphlets for educators, parents and children. It also publishes the booklet, *Educators, Schools and Child Abuse,* available for $1.50 per copy from the committee at P.O. Box 2866, Chicago, Illinois 60690.

The National Center on Child Abuse and Neglect also provides publications and resource materials at P.O. Box 1182, Washington, D.C. 20013.

Although child abuse is perceived to be a problem that primarily affects the disadvantaged, social-service agencies stress that child abuse cuts across all social, economic and racial lines. We as educators have a responsibility—one that can save lives.[1]

ENDNOTES

Megay-Nespoli, Karen: "Child Abuse and Neglect: What Educators Should Know," *Today's Catholic Educator* V.22 No. 8. May/June 1989. pp. 48–49.

National Committee for Prevention of Child Abuse: *Educators, School and Child Abuse.* Chicago, NCPCA 1986.

National Education Association: *Child Abuse and Neglect: A Teacher's Handbook for Detection, Reporting and Classroom Management,* West Haven, N.E.A., 1987.

Chapter Nineteen

EDUCATIONAL RESOURCES—
HOW AND WHERE TO GET HELP

"HELP! I need somebody.
HELP! Not just anybody.
HELP! You know I need someone.
H E L P !"   The Beatles

Everyone can benefit from some help now and then. In the field of education there's a wealth of valuable information to help teachers strengthen and fine tune their skills. The key is knowing where to find these resources. The first place to look is within the school walls.

Inside the School

Peers

Other classroom teachers can be a valuable asset to a new teacher. They are already established in the school and know the "ins and outs." They have practical advice to share: how to get organized, how to handle paper work, disciplinary problems, parents, supervisors and even curriculum ideas that have worked or backfired. They can often save you hours of work, just for the asking. You can begin by getting to know the faculty. You will find that many teachers are eager to help you once you break the ice:

1. Have lunch in the teacher's room, not at your desk. Join in the discussion.
2. Attend teacher workshops or inservice programs and ask questions.
3. Faculty meetings are also an excellent opportunity to meet fellow teachers. Don't bolt out the door after the meeting, stay for refreshments—its worth those few extra minutes.

167

Principal or Supervisor

Many teachers are afraid to ask their Principal for help. They are concerned that the Principal will think they are unqualified or can't handle the job. This is a common misconception.

The Principal is often perceived as the "enemy." You must remember that the Principal started out in a classroom much like yours. Believe it or not they understand the challenges you face during the first year. Come to your Principal with your problems. It is far better to hear it straight from the teacher than from some irate parents. Let your Principal know that you are trying and progressing. They like to hear good news too. You'll find out that the Principal is not the "enemy," but someone who cares—someone whose valuable experience can help you be a better teacher.

Mentoring

Mentor has come to mean an experienced and trusted counselor. Mentoring Intern Programs are very popular throughout the country. These programs match beginning teachers and experienced colleagues in a confidential helping relationship. The goal is to help ease the new teacher's entrance into the teaching profession. If you are interested, check with your supervisor. If there is no such program, you may want to ask one of your colleagues to be your mentor. Keep in mind that the key to a good mentoring relationship is confidentiality. The results may surprise you both.

Outside the School

Workshops and Inservice Courses

Your district may offer numerous workshops or inservice programs, especially designed for new teachers. Some may be required, others may not. Decide to take one or two a semester. They often provide a wealth of ideas and materials that can be used in the classroom.

University

Where better to gain more knowledge and skills than the University? Look through the Bulletin; select a course that sounds interesting. It doesn't need to be an education course; it can be for enjoyment or to begin a Master's Program. Whatever you decide the knowledge you gain will make you a better teacher.

Teacher Centers

Many districts have at least one Teacher Center. It is usually centrally located and housed in one of the schools.

Teacher Centers have computers, reference materials, books, pamphlets, guides, texts, games and teacher made materials. All of these materials can be used at the Center and some can be borrowed to use in your classroom.

Teacher Stores

Teacher stores contain everything you could dream of to fill a classroom. They have classroom furnishings, playground equipment, music and art supplies, bulletin board materials, maps, globes, science equipment, math manipulatives, games, books and audio/visual equipment. Ask a colleague for directions to the nearest store.

Teacher Organizations

You may want to consider joining one of these organizations. Belonging to a professional association can enhance your knowledge enormously. Consult your local library for a list of teacher organizations that are active in your city or state:

American Federation of Teachers
555 New Jersey Avenue N.W.
Washington, D.C. 20001

Council for Exceptional Children
1920 Association Drive
Reston, Virginia 22091

International Reading Association
P.O. Box 8139
800 Barkdale Road
Newark, Delaware 19711

Modern Language Association of America
62 Fifth Avenue
New York, New York 10011

Music Teachers National Association
408 Carew Tower
Cincinnati, Ohio 45202

National Art Educators Association
1916 Association Drive
Reston, Virginia 22091

National Association of Bilingual Education
BESL Center
100 Franklin Street
New Holland, Pennsylvania 17557

National Association for Education of Young Children
1834 Connecticut Avenue
Washington, D.C. 20009

National Council of Teachers of English
1111 Kenyon Road
Urbana, Illinois 61801

National Council of Teachers of Math
1906 Association Drive
Reston, Virginia 22091

National Education Association
1201 16th Street NW
Washington, D.C. 20036

National Middle School Association
P.O. Box 968
Fairborn, Ohio 45324

National Science Teachers Association
1742 Connecticut Avenue NW
Washington, D.C. 20009

Educational Journals

You may want to peruse several of these journals at the University library and when you find one or two you like, you may want to subscribe.

Arithmetic Teacher
1906 Association Drive
Reston, Virginia 22091

Written for teachers K–8. Allows educators to exchange ideas and techniques for teaching mathematics.

Creative Classroom
Children's Television Workshop
1 Lincoln Plaza
New York, New York 10023

Hands on activities magazine for elementary school teachers.

Educational Leadership
1250 North Pitt Street
Alexandria, Virginia 22314-1403

This journal addresses curriculum, instruction, supervision and leadership in education.

Gifted Child Today
P.O. Box 6448
Mobile, Alabama 36660

This educational journal is for parents and teachers of the gifted. Includes some research, and articles addressing practical classroom strategies.

Instructor
730 Broadway
New York, New York 10003

An educational magazine for elementary and middle school teachers. Includes effective teaching activities and strategies, art activities, new ideas and teaching devices.

Learning '93
Springhouse Corporation
1111 Bethlehem Pike
Springhouse, Pennsylvania 19477

Professional publication for teachers K–8. Articles include classroom techniques, materials, philosophies and personal teaching experiences.

Mailbox
The Educational Center, Inc.
1607 Battleground Avenue
P.O. Box 9753
Greensboro, North Carolina 27429

Hands on magazine includes: teaching units, reproducible worksheets, art activities, bulletin board ideas, awards and patterns and management tips.

SchoolDays
P.O. Box 2853
Torrance, California 90509-2853

Magazine of practical ideas for primary teachers. Thematic units, cooperative learning, manipulative math, bulletin boards, science and idea exchange are featured.

Teaching Pre K–8
40 Richards Avenue
7th Floor
Norwalk, Connecticut 06854

A magazine for teachers of Pre school–8 that describes new classroom practices and new approaches. Classroom tested ideas and techniques.

Today's Catholic Teacher
2451 East River Road
Dayton, Ohio 45489

An educational magazine featuring practical articles on early childhood and elementary education. Topics include: creative teaching, testing, computer education, faculty and parent/teacher relationships.

Books About Teaching

If you like to read about teaching and the experiences other teachers have had, here are a few books you might enjoy reading:

Appelman, Diane and McClear, Johanna: *Teacher, the Children are Here: A Guide for Teachers of Elementary Grades.* Scott Foresman, 1988.

Ashton-Warner, Sylvia,: *Teacher.* Simon and Schuster, 1963.

Bluestein, Jane Ph.D.: *Being a Successful Teacher.* ISS Publications, 1988.

Christopher, Cindy: *Nuts and Bolts: Survival Guide For Teachers.* Technomic, 1992.

Craig, Eleanor: *P.S. You're Not Listening.* Baron, 1972.

Daniels, Steven: *How 2 Gerbils, 20 Goldfish, 200 Games, 2000 Books and I Taught Them How to Read.* Westminster, 1972.

Gross, Beatrice and Gross, Ronald: *Will It Grow in a Classroom.* Delacourte, 1974.

Herndon, James: *The Way It Spozed to Be.* Simon and Schuster, 1970.

Holt, John: *What Do I Do Monday?* Dell, 1972.
Kohl, Herbert: *36 Children.* New American Library, 1967.
Sachar, Emily: *Shut Up and Let the Lady Teach.* Posiden, 1991.

Computer Networks

There is one last resource to mention, Computer Networks. The purpose of computer networks is to support and encourages first year teachers. Harvard Graduate School of Education initiated a network called Beginning Teacher Computer Network in 1987. The network links graduates of Harvard teacher education programs in their first year of teaching across the United States. Harvard faculty and staff, some second year teachers and other invited guests are also members of this network.[2]

Here's how it works. The network is small and requires using a personal computer, modem and a single telephone line.

In order to receive advice and suggestions about some challenging aspect of teaching, the network user must present a question or brief description of problems.

The community of other first year teacher and faculty members respond to questions or problems. Sometimes they offer advice, other times support.

The network creates a supportive, community of learners who actively consult with one another to minimize problems. Who knows, there may be a computer network in your future. For further information you may want to read the following articles:

Merseth, Katherine K.: "First Aid for First Year Teachers." Phi Delta Kappa. May, 1992.

Merseth, Katherine: "Computer Networks for New Teachers." Harvard Education Letter. July/August 1989.

With all of this information right at your fingertips you can't help but have a successful first year, and many years to come, as a teacher.

ENDNOTES

1. Lennon, John and McCartney, Paul, "H E L P !" BMI, New York 1966.
2. Merseth, Katherine K.: "First Aid for First Year Teachers" Phi Delta Kappa. May, 1992 pp. 678–683.

Chapter Twenty

SCHOOL CALENDAR IN REVIEW

September

Before School Starts

A. Faculty Meeting—You will meet the Principal, school secretary and other staff members. You will receive information about:
1. Class assignment.
2. School hours and dismissal times.
3. Schedules for recess and lunch hours.
4. Fire drill procedures.
5. Instructional time for academic subjects.
6. Duty roster for bus duty, recess and lunch.
7. School rules and procedures for the yard and lunch room.
8. Procedures for new entrants.
9. Attendance and Lunch Card procedures.
10. Rainy day procedures.
11. Plan Book and substitute plans.
12. Ordering supplies and textbooks.
13. Audio/visual aids.
14. Copy of class list, classroom keys and record cards for your class.

B. Your Classroom—Things to do in your classroom before the students arrive:
1. Move furniture and desks—think through traffic patterns.
2. Place your desk where it does not obstruct blackboard space.
3. Have extra desks ready for new entrants.
4. Set up a desk and chairs where an adult can work one on one with a student.
5. Create a "time out" corner.
6. Decorate your bulletin boards.
7. Inventory your educational materials.
8. Make your seating plan.
9. Peruse the student's records.

10. Check your audio/visual equipment and outlets.
11. Set up filing system for faculty notes and other pertinent papers.
12. Order your supplies and textbooks.
13. Tour the school facility.
14. Make a friend.
15. Tab your teacher's manuals by chapters for easy access.
16. Create a filing system for dittos.
17. Label shelves—things can be returned much easier by students, parent helpers or substitutes.

C. Lesson Plans
1. Over plan more than you will need.
2. Plan schedule and be flexible with other teachers who need to change your schedule.
3. Alternate quiet and active lessons.
4. Keep things simple and build on their successes.

The First Day of School

A. Before the Students Arrive:
1. Arrive early and get yourself settled.
2. Relax—You'll be great!
3. Check your room for any last minute changes.
4. Write your name on the blackboard.
5. Prepare to meet your first class.

B. Meeting your Class:
1. Greet your class with a smile.
2. Answer parent questions or direct them to the office.
3. Bring your class to their classroom.
4. Seat the children according to your plan.
5. Introduce yourself.
6. Show them where the closet is for coats, book bags and lunch boxes, you'll explain procedures later.
7. Take attendance.
8. Talk about routines and rules.
9. Break up the day with movement activities.
10. Don't forget to read a story.
11. Tour the school with your class.
12. Answer all their questions.
13. Sing a song.
14. Distribute information to go home and dismiss your class.

The First Week of School

A. Getting into a routine.
   1. Set standards and practice them.
   2. Begin to study your children.
   3. Start files for each student for their work and tests.
   4. Read cumulative records, last report card, and health card.
   5. Administer an informal reading inventory to help you decide placement in a reading group.
   6. Begin anecdotal records.
   7. Share information with parents, open the lines of communication. Ask for volunteers to help in the classroom.
   8. Prepare your notes for Back to School Night.

The Rest of the School Year

A. October:
   1. Recruit class mothers or parents to help with trips and parties.
   2. Incorporate "pull out" programs.
   3. Post your daily schedule.
   4. Set up your substitute folder.
   5. Find out policy on Halloween parties and costumes.
   6. Begin planning your first party.
   7. Begin planning a class trip for early December.
B. November:
   1. Report card time—get samples, read all materials and review past report card.
   2. Start your cards early.
   3. Make your comments count—use clear, simple language.
   4. Conferences will soon follow.
   5. Plan ahead to get through the conference period.
   6. Make an index card for each child and the pertinent information you want to share with the parents.
   7. Set up conference schedule to meet with each parent.
   8. Keep a record of suggestions or plans made by you or the parent. Follow through on all plans. Keep the index cards in a file along with any notations you have made.
   9. Discuss upcoming trip with your class.
   10. Thanksgiving—Plan activities, art projects and special books to share about this holiday.

11. Plan and order supplies necessary for holiday gifts.
12. If you are giving holiday gifts to your students, find out what other teachers do and order them early to ensure they will arrive before Christmas.

C. December:
1. Finish up last minute details for class trip. Be sure to collect all permission slips and to collect all money.
2. Class Trip—have a great time!
3. Begin working on children's holiday gifts for their parents. Be sensitive to all religions and family backgrounds. Some have extended families and may want to make more than one. Have plenty of extras on hand.
4. Plan your Holiday Party.
5. Tidy up the classroom for the Holiday Recess.

D. January:
1. Time to call an early conference to discuss possible hold overs.
2. Time for health check—height, weight, vision.
3. Time to check your student's addresses and telephone numbers.
4. Begin planning a class trip for March.

E. February:
1. Valentine's Day—Will you have cards? If so, a class list will help your students and ask that they send one to each child so no feelings are hurt.
2. Begin to plan your class play.
3. Complete last minute details for your class trip.
4. Open School Week.

F. March:
1. Class trip.
2. Report cards will be due this month.
3. Followed by parent-teacher conferences.
4. Practice, practice, practice for your class play.
5. Celebrate Saint Patrick's Day with some Irish Soda Bread and a little dance called the jig.
6. Your First Class Play. Break a leg!
7. Celebrate with a cast party.

G. April:
1. Spring is here. Celebrate all holidays—Easter, Passover and others.
2. Plan your celebrations—will you have an egg hunt?
3. Fill out cumulative records except for last minute additions.

    4. Prepare for Standardized Tests.
    5. Plan minimal lessons during this testing time.
    6. Plan your last class trip for May or early June.
H. May:
    1. Complete the cumulative folder before you begin the report cards.
    2. Start to pack away classroom materials that you will not be using the rest of the year.
    3. Complete details of your last class trip of the year.
    4. Have a quick conference with parents who want to help their child over the summer.
    5. Evaluate the school year—what went well, what would you change or do differently. Make some notes to refer to in late August.
I. June:
    1. Complete report cards, cumulative records, health cards and conferences.
    2. Complete awards, certificates, and diplomas.
    3. Plan your end of the year party. Have it early rather than the last day.
    4. Save incomplete workbooks to pass on to the next teacher or to be completed over the summer and returned to next teacher.
    5. Send home ideas for summer practice and review.
    6. Write thank you notes to all class mothers and parent helpers.
    7. Clean up classroom, take down decorations and label them for future use, label and store audio/visual equipment.
    8. Place all decorations for the fall in a box with everything you need to set up your room: alphabet, number line, calendar, bulletin board paper and bordette.
    9. Have your party.
    10. Keep a running list of materials you want to buy, make or collect over the summer.
    11. Congratulations, you made it through your first year!

Miscellaneous:

    1. Keep the following in your closet:
        a. comfortable shoes
        b. umbrella
        c. sneakers for P. E.
        d. whistle

e. sweater
f. smock
g. change of clothes and extra pantihose
h. personal hygiene items

RULES FOR TEACHERS

1. Teachers each day will fill lamps, clean chimneys and trim wicks.
2. Each teacher will bring a bucket of water and scuttle of coal for the day's session.
3. Make your pens carefully. You may whittle nibs to the individual tastes of the pupil.
4. Men teachers may take on evening each week for courting purposes or two evenings a week if they go to church regularly.
5. After ten hours of school, the teacher should spend the remaining time reading the Bible or other good books.
6. Women teachers who marry or engage in unseemly conduct will be dismissed.
7. Every teacher should lay aside from each pay a goodly sum of his earnings for his benefit during declining years, so that he will not be a burden on society.
8. Any teacher who smokes, uses liquor in any form, frequents pool or public halls or gets shaved in a barber shop will give good reason to suspect his worth, intentions, integrity and honesty.
9. The teacher who performs his labors faithfully and without fault for five years will be given an increase of twenty-five cents per week in his pay, providing the Board of Education approves.

Posted by a Principal in New York City, 1872

From *America's Best Classrooms* by Daniel Seymour and Terry Seymour. Reprinted by permission of Peterson's, 202 Carnegie Center, P.O. Box 2123, Princeton, N.J. 08543. (800-338-3282)

IN CLOSING

The first year of teaching is difficult, all your thoughts, words and actions will revolve around school. There is so much to do, to learn, to prepare and assimilate. You will spend endless hours working with students, teachers, administrators and parents. At times it seems endless, but take heart. It does get better and easier after that first year is behind you.

Think back to when you were in school. Wasn't there one teacher you remember more than the rest. Why does that teacher stand out in your mind? What made that teacher different from the rest?

Now it is your turn to go out there and be that special teacher. You can be the teacher that they will long remember.

You are about to embark on an exciting, challenging, and rewarding teaching career.

Congratulations
and
Best of Luck

AN INVITATION

Now that you are an expert, you can help to make the next edition of this book more comprehensive and useful to other new teachers. Send: helpful hints, anecdotes, examples, suggestions and criticisms. Tell me what worked and what didn't work for you. If your input is useful, it will appear in the next edition of this book.

Write me please:

Mrs. Karen Megay-Nespoli
93 Philadelphia Avenue
Massapequa Park, N.Y. 11762

BIBLIOGRAPHY

1. Alexander, Carole: "Presentation Skills." Staff Development Workshop. Massapequa Union Free School District. Massapequa, New York, 1991.
2. Alexander, Kern: *School Law.* St. Paul, West, 1980.
3. American Federation of Teachers: "Your Career as An Educational Para-Professional." Washington, D.C., AFT, 1987.
4. American Medical Association: *Home Medical Advisor.* New York, Random House, 1988.
5. American Red Cross: *Standard First Aid and Personal Safety.* Garden City, Doubleday, 1988.
6. Anderson, Patricia and Laminack, Lester: "Motivation: The Missing Ingredient." *Early Years,* 18:37, 1985.
7. Bartlett, L.: "Don't Mix: A Critical Review." *Journal of Law and Education,* 16:155–15, 1987.
8. Bartlett, L.: *Student Press and Distribution Issues, Rights and Responsibilities.* Reston, NASSP, 1987.
9. Borders, Earl Jr.: *The Bus Trip Handbook.* New Jersey, Home Run Press, 1985.
10. Brisson, Lynn: *3-D Bulletin Boards.* New York, Fantail, 1989.
11. Brown, James, Lewis, Richard and Harcleroad, Fred: A V Instruction: *Technology, Media and Methods.* New York, McGraw Hill, 1977.
12. Brown, Susan: "What To Look for When Studying Children." Libertyville, Media Workshop, 1971.
13. Butler, Arlene Kay: *Traveling With Children and Enjoying It.* Chester, Globe Pequot, 1991.
14. Cantor, Lee: "Homework Without Tears." Instructor XCVIII:29–30, 1988.
15. Center for Disease Control: "Guidelines for Effective School Health Education to Prevent the Spread of AIDS, Morbitity, Mortality." Weekly Report, January, 1988.
16. Clewett, Anne S.: "Discipline as Teaching Rather than Punishment." *Young Children,* XLIII: 26–31, 1988.
17. Collinwood, Gerry: *Ideas for Learning Centers.* Hansford, Kings County Curriculum Services, 1977.
18. Cornett, Claudia E.: "What You Should Know About Teaching and Learning Styles." Phi Delta Kappa, 1983.
19. Dallmann, Martha: *Teaching the Language Arts in the Elementary School.* Dubuque, Wm. C. Brown, 1976.

20. Dockterman, David and Bowman, Sally: "Why We Should Do "real things" with Computers. *American Teacher,* 74:2, 1989.

21. Dougherty, Anne: *Beginnings: A Guide for New Teachers.* Coronado, Beginnings, 1988.

22. Dunn, Rita and Dunn, Kenneth: *Teaching Students Through Their Individual Learning Styles: A Practical Approach.* Reston, 1978.

23. Ehrlich, Virginia: *Gifted Children; A Guide for Parents and Teachers.* Monroe, Trillium, 1989.

24. Engel v Vitale, 370 US 421, 82 S.Ct. 1261 (1962).

25. Freeman, Lois M.: *Parties for Children.* New York, Golden, 1964.

26. Fitzpatrick, Jean Grasso: "Take This Homework Test..." *Working Mother,* January 1991.

27. Flynn, Jean: "Preparation for the First Day." Chicago, Continental, 1973.

28. Gault 387 US1 (1967).

29. Goss v Lopez 419 US 565, 42 (1987).

30. Guilford, J.P.: *Intelligence, Creativity and Their Educational Implications.* San Diego, Knapp, 1968.

31. Heinig, Ruth: *Creative Drama for the Classroom Teacher K–3.* New Jersey, Prentice-Hall, 1987.

32. Kamiya, Arthur: *Elementary Teacher's Handbook of Indoor and Outdoor Games.* New York, Parker, 1985.

33. Karlin, Robert: *Teaching Elementary Reading: Principals and Strategies.* New York, Harcourt, Brace, Jovanovich, 1971.

34. Kirk, Samuel and Gallagher, James: *Educating Exceptional Children.* Boston, Houghton Mifflin, 1972.

35. Klawetter, Pamela: "Mini Centers." *Instructor,* 90:64–71, 1980.

36. Koop, Everett C.: *Surgeon General's Report on AIDS.* Washington, D.C., Human Services, 1986.

37. Kounin, Jacob: *Discipline and Group Management in Classrooms.* New York, Holt, Rinehart and Winston, 1970.

38. Long, James, Frye, Virginia H. and Long, Elizabeth W.: *Making It 'Till Friday: A Guide to Successful Classroom Management.* New Jersey, Princton Book, 1989.

39. McCaslin, Nellie: *Creative Drama in the Classroom.* White Plains, Longman, 1990.

40. Martin, R.: *Legal Issues in Behavior Modification.* Champaign, Research Press, 1975.

41. Massapequa Union Free School District: *Curriculum Guide on AIDS.* Massapequa Union Free School District, Massapequa, 1987.

42. Megay-Nespoli, Karen: "Child Abuse and Neglect: What Educators Need to Know." *Today's Catholic Educator,* 22:48–49, 1989.

43. Megay-Nespoli, Karen: "Effective Classroom Management." *Today's Catholic Educator,* 17:37, 1984.

44. Merseth, Katherine K. "First Aid for First Year Teachers." Bloomington, Phi Delta Kappa, 73:678–683, 1992.

45. Meyers, Ellen (Ed.): *New Teachers Handbook.* New York, Impact II, 1988.

46. Morrissey, Virginia: "Law Refresher." New York City Board of Education, District 24, Queens, 1980.

47. National Committee for Prevention of Child Abuse: *Educators, Schools and Child Abuse.* Chicago, NCPCA, 1987.
48. National Education Association: *Child Abuse and Neglect: A Teacher's Handbook for Detection, Reporting and Classroom Management.* Washington, D.C., NEA, 1986.
49. National Education Association: *Conference Time for Teachers and Parents.* Washington, D.C., NEA, 1984.
50. National School Public Relations Association: *Standardized, Aptitude and Achievement Testing.* Arlington, NYSYUT, 1978.
51. Noll, Victor H. and Scannell, Dale P.: *Introduction to Educational Measurement.* Boston, Houghton, 1972.
52. Nolte, M.C.: "Before You Take a Paddling to Court, Read This Corporal Punishment Advice." *American School Board Journal,* 35:173–227, 1987.
53. Ohles, John: *Introduction to Teaching.* New York, Random House, 1970.
54. ParaProfessional and School Related Personnel: *Employee You Have a Tough Job.* Washington, D.C., AFT, 1989.
55. ParaProfessional and School Related Personnel: *Safe and Healthy Schools: The School Employees Guide to First Aid and Health Problems.* Washington, D.C., AFT, 1984.
56. People v Jackson 65 Misc. 2d. 909 319 NYS 2d. 731 (1971).
57. Portnoy, Stanford and Portnoy, Joan: *How to Take Great Trips With Your Kids.* Boston, Harvard Common, 1983.
58. Prizzi, E. and Hoffman, J.: *Interactive Bulletin Boards.* Chicago, Fearon, 1984.
59. Rauth, Marilyn: "Research on Effective Classroom Management for the Beginning of the School Year." Washington, D.C., AFT, 1985.
60. Rosen, Carol and Rudnick, Phyllis: *Teacher to Teacher.* New York, Harvin, 1987.
61. School District of Abington Township v Shempp and Murray v Curlett 374 US 203, 83 S.Ct. 1560 (1963).
62. Sparzo, Frank J.: *Preparing Better Teacher Made Tests: A Practical Guide.* Bloomington, Phi Delta Kappa, 1990.
63. Steinberg, Adria (Ed.): "Organizing Classes by Ability." Cambridge, *Harvard Education Letter,* III:1–4, 1987.
64. Steinberg, Adria (Ed.): "Unpopular Children." Cambridge, *Harvard Education Letter,* V:1–3, 1989.
65. Stoops, Emery, Rafferty, Max and Johnson, Russel: *Handbook of Educational Administration: A Guide for the Practitioner.* Boston, Allyn and Bacon, 1975.
66. Tingey-Michaelis, Carol: "Day One! How to Handle That All Important First Day of School." *Early Years,* 15:37–38, 1984.
67. Tinker v Des Moines Independent School District 393 US 503, 89 S.Ct. 733 (1969).
68. Wankelman, Willard and Wigg, Phillip: *A Handbook of Arts and Crafts.* Dubuque, Wm. C. Brown, 1985.
69. Wolf, Dennie Palmer and Mitchell, Ruth: "Student Portfolios—Good-bye to Multiple Choice?" *American Teacher,* 76:2, 1992.

INDEX